I0108794

# 1500 POSITIVE AFFIRMATIONS FOR WOMEN AND MEN:

## Take advantage of the power of positive thinking, attract money, happiness, love and success.

Ricardo Vazquez

Copyright © 2025


eBook ISBN: 979-8-89965-135-9

Paperback ISBN: 979-8-89965-133-5

Hardcover ISBN: 979-8-89965-132-8


All © Reserved. Any unauthorized reprint or use of this material is strictly prohibited. No part of this book may be reproduced or transmitted in any form or by any means, electronic or mechanical, including photocopying, recording, or by any information storage and retrieval system without express written permission from the author.

All reasonable attempts have been made to verify the accuracy of the information provided in this publication. Nevertheless, the author assumes no responsibility for any errors and/or omissions.

**To my beloved wife and son,**

*To my beloved wife, Luz, whose unwavering support and boundless love have been the light guiding me through every chapter of life. Your strength inspires me, and you fill my days with joy.*

*To my precious son, Ricardo, may this book inspire you to dream big and embrace your own story. You are my greatest adventure, and I hope you always know how deeply you are loved.*

*This book is dedicated to all those who seek a path to self-discovery, personal growth, and unwavering positivity. May these affirmations provide you with the inspiration and motivation to cultivate a life filled with love, abundance, and resilience. Let this guide empower you to embrace your individuality, nurture your well-being, and create the fulfilling life you deserve.*

# Table of Contents

Introduction

Cultivating a Positive Mindset Through Affirmations ..........2

Chapter 1

Morning Affirmations for a Fresh Start. ...............................5

Chapter 2

Building Confidence at Work ..............................................18

Chapter 3

Embarking on a Healthier Lifestyle ...................................33

Chapter 4

Nurturing Positive Relationships .......................................49

Chapter 5

Achieving Abundance and Success .....................................66

Chapter 6

Cultivating a Mindset of Resilience....................................83

Chapter 7

Embracing Change and New Beginnings ...........................98

Chapter 8

Fostering Creativity and Inspiration ................................115

Chapter 9

Nurturing Self-Acceptance and Love ...................132

Chapter 10

Gratitude and Reflection ...............................149

Chapter 11

Enhancing Emotional Well-Being ......................166

Chapter 12

Unlocking Your Inner Potential........................183

Chapter 13

Creating Harmonious Environments....................199

Chapter 14

Cultivating a Growth Mindset .........................216

Chapter 15

Celebrating Love and Life .............................233

EPILOGUE

The Journey Continues .................................250

# Introduction

## Cultivating a Positive Mindset Through Affirmations

# Introduction

## Cultivating a Positive Mindset Through Affirmations

In today's fast-paced world, the pressures of daily life can often lead to stress, doubt, and feelings of inadequacy. As we navigate through various challenges, it becomes increasingly important to cultivate a positive mindset that not only enhances our mental well-being but also enriches our overall quality of life. One powerful tool for achieving this is the practice of self-affirmations—simple yet profound statements that encourage self-love, gratitude, resilience, and personal growth.

Self-affirmations serve as essential reminders of our inherent worth and potential. They enable us to replace negative self-talk with constructive, uplifting messages that resonate with our true selves. By integrating affirmations into our daily routines, we create a positive feedback loop that reinforces self-acceptance and inspires us to pursue our goals with confidence and determination. Research in the psychology of happiness highlights the transformative effects of maintaining a positive mindset. When we practice gratitude and affirmations, we nurture a sense of well-being that ripples into all aspects of our lives, fostering resilience, creativity, and deeper connections with others.

This book is a journey through fifteen empowering themes, each designed to elevate your mindset and encourage personal transformation. From starting your mornings on a positive note to embracing change and nurturing meaningful relationships, these affirmations are crafted to support you in every facet of your life. By repeatedly affirming your strengths, potential, and self-worth, you will enhance your emotional resilience and open yourself up to new possibilities.

As you work through each chapter, take the time to reflect on the affirmations that resonate with you. Allow these powerful words to serve as guiding principles on your journey toward self-discovery, empowerment, and fulfillment. Remember, every affirmation is a step toward creating the life you desire—one infused with positivity, gratitude, and abundant success.

Let this book be a source of inspiration and motivation as you embark on a transformative journey of self-acceptance, gratitude, and personal growth. With each affirmation you embrace, you are not only nurturing your well-being, but you are also cultivating a brighter, more fulfilling future for yourself. Together, let's unlock the potential that lies within and celebrate the beauty of our unique journeys!

# 1

## Morning Affirmations for a Fresh Start.

Focus on setting a positive tone for the day ahead with affirmations that encourage gratitude and optimism.

# Chapter 1

## Morning Affirmations for a Fresh Start.

Focus on setting a positive tone for the day ahead with affirmations that encourage gratitude and optimism.

Mornings hold a special power; they set the tone for the day ahead and can significantly influence our mindset and productivity. The first moments after waking up are critical, as they offer an opportunity to cultivate a positive mindset that can carry us through the day. Reading and reciting morning affirmations for a fresh start is an effective practice for aligning our thoughts with optimism and gratitude.

Incorporating affirmations into your morning routine can create a ripple effect of positivity that enhances your emotional well-being. By focusing on uplifting and inspiring words each day, you program your mind to approach challenges with strength and resilience. Morning affirmations encourage you to cultivate a sense of gratitude for the opportunities that lie ahead, helping to shift your perspective from negativity and worry to one of hope and possibility.

The benefits of engaging in this practice extend beyond the morning hours; they can influence our interactions with others, our decision-making processes, and our overall sense of fulfillment. Each affirmation serves as a gentle reminder of your worth, potential, and capacity for growth. By starting each day with intention and self-love, you empower yourself to embrace whatever comes your way.

As you read through these daily affirmations, take a moment to reflect on their meaning and how they resonate with your unique journey. Allow them to inspire you to embrace the day ahead with enthusiasm and positivity. Remember, your mindset shapes your reality, and by nurturing a habit of gratitude and optimism, you are laying the foundation for a joyful and fulfilling life. Let's embark on this journey together and make each morning a powerful step toward personal growth and fulfillment!

1. I am grateful for this new day and all the

possibilities it brings.

2. Today, I choose to focus on the positive.

3. I wake up motivated and excited for what today

will bring.

4. I attract joy and happiness into my life.

5. Today is filled with endless opportunities.

6. I embrace the day with a grateful heart.

7. I am worthy of all the good things that come my way today.

8. I choose to see the beauty in everything around me.

9. Today, I will make choices that empower me.

10. I am open to receiving love, success, and positivity today.

11. I radiate positive energy that attracts good things.

12. I am enough just as I am.

13. I welcome challenges as opportunities for growth.

14. Each moment of today holds the potential for joy.

15. I am thankful for my health and vitality.

16. I choose to let go of negativity and embrace positivity.

17. I have the power to create my own happiness today.

18. I am surrounded by love and support.

19. Today, I will take a step toward my dreams.

20. I focus on what I can control and let go of the rest.

21. I am capable of handling anything that comes my way.

22. I trust myself to make the best decisions today.

23. I celebrate my strengths and embrace my weaknesses.

24. I attract positive people into my life.

25. Today, I choose to be kind to myself and others.

26. I am grateful for the opportunities for growth that today presents.

27. I am confident in my abilities and skills.

28. I choose to see the good in every situation.

29. I am ready to face the day with courage and determination.

30. My heart is open to new possibilities.

31. I embrace change as a natural part of my journey.

32. I bring light and positivity into the world around me.

33. I am grateful for the lessons that life teaches me.

34. Today, I choose joy over fear.

35. I attract abundance and prosperity into my life.

36. I am worthy of success and happiness.

37. I wake up each day with a sense of purpose.

38. I am fiercely committed to my goals.

39. I encourage myself to take risks and grow from them.

40. I start this day with intention and focus.

41. I am grateful for my unique gifts and talents.

42. I trust the timing of my life and embrace each moment.

43. I am a magnet for positive experiences.

44. Today, I will practice focus and appreciation.

45. I am resilient and able to overcome any challenge.

46. I am filled with excitement for the day ahead.

47. I choose to focus on what makes me happy.

48. I am grateful for the love I receive and give.

49. I embrace my journey with an open heart and mind.

50. I have the power to create positive change in my life.

51. I welcome abundance in all its forms.

52. I foster a mindset of gratitude and appreciation.

53. I am surrounded by opportunities for success.

54. Today, I will express my creativity freely.

55. I am deserving of good things today and every day.

56. I cultivate a calm and peaceful mind.

57. I live my life with purpose and intent.

58. I am open to new ideas and perspectives.

59. I choose to let go of past grudges and move forward.

60. I am a source of positivity and inspiration for others.

61. I am grateful for each breath I take today.

62. I choose to love and accept myself unconditionally.

63. I take pride in my accomplishments, no matter how small.

64. I am capable of achieving my dreams and goals.

65. I surround myself with positive thoughts and actions.

66. I find joy in the little things today.

67. I trust in my journey and the path that lies ahead.

68. I am strong, capable, and resilient.

69. I am committed to my personal growth and development.

70. I embrace each day with an open heart.

71. I am grateful for the abundance that surrounds me.

72. My mindset is focused on success and positivity.

73. I am proud of who I am becoming.

74. I am in control of my emotions and reactions.

75. I approach the day with a sense of curiosity and adventure.

76. I choose to make a difference in the world.

77. My dreams are valid, and I will pursue them.

78. I am grateful for the support of my loved ones.

79. I awaken each day with a sense of wonder.

80. I am deserving of love, health, and happiness.

81. I focus on solutions, not problems.

82. I will make time for self-care and relaxation today.

83. I trust in my ability to overcome resistance

84. I am in tune with my emotions and honor my feelings.

85. I embrace my individuality and celebrate my uniqueness.

86. I am grateful for the lessons that challenges teach me.

87. I attract positive energy and leave negativity behind.

88. Every day is a new opportunity to grow and learn.

89. I am surrounded by beauty and inspiration.

90. I believe in my potential and abilities.

91. I approach the day with optimism and enthusiasm.

92. I will spread kindness and uplift others today.

93. I deserve to rest, recharge, and rejuvenate.

94. I choose to forgive myself and others for past mistakes.

95. I am filled with gratitude for the love in my life.

96. I will take small steps towards my biggest goals today.

97. I welcome peace and calm into my day.

98. I am open to receiving unexpected blessings.

99. I trust myself to make the right choices today.

100. I am excited to embrace all that today has to offer.

# 2

## Building Confidence at Work.

Affirmations designed to boost self-esteem and assertiveness, helping you tackle challenges and embrace opportunities in your career.

# Chapter 2

# Building Confidence at Work.

Affirmations designed to boost self-esteem and assertiveness, helping you tackle challenges and embrace opportunities in your career.

In today's fast-paced and competitive professional landscape, confidence plays a crucial role in unlocking our potential and achieving success. The ability to project self-assurance not only enhances our interactions with colleagues and superiors but also empowers us to seize opportunities and tackle challenges head-on. Building confidence at work is essential for career advancement, personal fulfillment, and overall job satisfaction.

The affirmations presented in this chapter are designed to bolster your self-esteem and assertiveness, providing you with the mental tools necessary to navigate the complexities of the workplace. By nurturing a confident mindset, you can transform your approach to challenges, viewing them as stepping stones to personal and professional growth rather than obstacles to be feared.

Daily affirmations serve as powerful reminders of your capabilities and worth. They encourage you to acknowledge your strengths, embrace your unique contributions, and assert your voice in any situation. As you integrate these affirmations into your routine, you will cultivate a sense of inner strength that enables you to express your ideas boldly and confidently.

Moreover, fostering confidence at work enhances your relationships with colleagues and clients, allowing for more effective collaboration and communication. When you believe in yourself, you inspire trust and respect from others, creating a positive and empowering work environment.

As you delve into this collection of affirmations, take the time to reflect on their significance in your professional journey. Embrace the notion that confidence is not merely an innate trait but a skill that can be developed and strengthened over time. By practicing these affirmations, you will not only elevate your self-esteem but also unlock new opportunities for success and fulfillment in your career. Let's embark on this journey together and embrace the confident, capable professional that lies within you!

1. I am capable and confident in my abilities.

2. I bring unique skills and talents to my workplace.

3. I embrace challenges as opportunities to grow.

4. I trust my instincts and make decisions with

confidence.

5. I am a valuable member of my team.

6. My contributions are important and appreciated.

7. I am a leader in my own right.

8. I handle criticism gracefully and learn from it.

9. I express my ideas clearly and confidently.

10. I am open to feedback and use it for improvement.

11. I face difficulties with courage and resilience.

12. I am deserving of success in my career.

13. I celebrate my accomplishments, no matter how small.

14. I am proactive in my professional development.

15. I attract opportunities that align with my goals.

16. I communicate assertively and effectively.

17. My confidence shines through in all my interactions.

18. I am always learning and growing in my profession.

19. I inspire others with my confidence and dedication.

20. I believe in my potential and pursue my aspirations.

21. I am open to taking risks that lead to growth.

22. I handle workplace challenges with a positive mindset.

23. I set clear boundaries and stand up for myself.

24. I create a positive work environment through my attitude.

25. I am proud of my achievements and showcase them.

26. I approach each day with enthusiasm and determination.

27. I am committed to my goals and pursue them relentlessly.

28. I foster strong relationships based on respect and trust.

29. I visualize my success and take steps toward it.

30. I am a lifelong learner and welcome new knowledge.

31. I use my strengths to overcome obstacles.

32. I handle stress with grace and composure.

33. I am respected and valued by my colleagues.

34. I choose positivity and focus on solutions.

35. I confidently share my ideas in meetings and discussions.

36. I am adaptable and embrace change in my career.

37. I have the power to create my desired career path.

38. I approach conflicts with an open mind and heart.

39. I am fearless in pursuing my dreams and goals.

40. I take pride in my work and its impact.

41. I am surrounded by supportive and encouraging colleagues.

42. I cultivate a mindset of growth and possibility.

43. I acknowledge and appreciate my progress.

44. I am worthy of recognition and success.

45. I take calculated risks that expand my horizons.

46. I handle rejection with resilience and learn from it.

47. I communicate with clarity and confidence.

48. I embrace feedback as a tool for growth.

49. I am assertive in expressing my needs and wants.

50. I choose to rise above negativity in the workplace.

51. I am in control of my professional journey.

52. I act with integrity and authenticity in all I do.

53. I celebrate the achievements of my peers and support them.

54. I trust myself to navigate my career path successfully.

55. I maintain a healthy work-life balance that fuels my confidence.

56. I am open to new challenges that develop my skills.

57. I take initiative and lead projects with confidence.

58. I am prepared to handle any situation that arises.

59. I am influential and inspire others with my vision.

60. I seek out mentors who encourage my growth and success.

61. I attract positive opportunities in my career journey.

62. I approach tasks with enthusiasm and a can-do attitude.

63. I am a problem solver who finds creative solutions.

64. I voice my opinions respectfully and assertively.

65. I recognize my worth and advocate for myself.

66. I collaborate effectively with my team and add value.

67. I am grateful for each learning opportunity in my career.

68. I visualize my future success and take steps toward it.

69. I let go of limiting beliefs and embrace my potential.

70. I am focused on my goals and work toward them daily.

71. I am confident in my ability to lead and influence.

72. I embrace challenges as stepping stones to success.

73. I recognize and overcome self-doubt with positivity.

74. I approach my work with passion and purpose.

75. I am competent and excel in my job responsibilities.

76. I am worthy of the achievements I strive for.

77. I contribute to a collaborative and supportive workplace.

78. I set ambitious goals and work diligently to achieve them.

79. I tackle tough tasks with confidence and determination.

80. I embrace constructive criticism as an opportunity for growth.

81. I balance humility with confidence in my abilities.

82. I lead by example and inspire others to do their best.

83. I continually seek personal and professional improvement.

84. I am surrounded by an empowering and motivating community.

85. I embrace my unique journey and its lessons.

86. I am proud of my career choices and their impact.

88. I approach every challenge with a positive mindset.

89. I trust my skills and knowledge to achieve my goals.

90. I actively seek opportunities for collaboration and growth.

91. I maintain a confident posture and demeanor in all situations.

92. I am my own greatest advocate and support.

93. I attract success through my hard work and determination.

94. I focus on solutions rather than dwelling on problems.

95. I celebrate my unique contributions to my team.

96. I am committed to creating a positive impact in my workplace.

97. I cultivate meaningful connections with my colleagues.

98. I embrace my worth and confidently promote my achievements.

99. I am open to new experiences that enhance my professional life.

100. I make decisions with clarity and confidence, knowing I will succeed.

# 3

## Embarking on a Healthier Lifestyle.

Positive affirmations aimed at motivation for fitness, healthy eating, and holistic well-being.

# Chapter 3

## Embarking on a Healthier Lifestyle.

Positive affirmations aimed at motivation for fitness, healthy eating, and holistic well-being.

Our health is our most valuable asset, and nurturing it should be a priority in our lives. Embarking on a healthier lifestyle is not just a goal; it is a transformative journey that encompasses physical fitness, balanced nutrition, and holistic well-being. It is about making conscious choices that empower us to live life to the fullest and enjoy the vitality we deserve.

The affirmations in this chapter are designed to motivate and inspire you on your journey to better health. Each positive statement serves as a powerful reminder of your commitment to self-care and well-being, helping you cultivate a positive mindset towards fitness and nutrition. By repeating these affirmations, you will reinforce your intention to make healthier choices that align with your values and aspirations.

Choosing to lead a healthier lifestyle goes beyond physical appearance; it is about fostering a deep sense of connection between your mind, body, and spirit. When you prioritize your health, you enhance your energy levels, mental clarity, and emotional balance. These affirmations encourage you to embrace the beauty of holistic well-being, reminding you that true health encompasses not just exercise and diet, but also emotional resilience and self-love.

As you engage with these affirmations, take the time to reflect on what health means to you personally. Visualize your goals, whether they involve adopting a new fitness routine, embracing healthier eating habits, or nurturing your mental well-being. Allow these affirmations to guide you toward a lifestyle filled with vitality, joy, and fulfillment.

Remember, embarking on a healthier lifestyle is a journey, not a destination. Each small step you take contributes to your overall well-being. By incorporating these affirmations into your daily routine, you empower yourself to make choices that lead to a healthier, happier, and more vibrant life. Let's embark on this transformative journey together and celebrate every positive step along the way!

1. I am committed to nurturing my body and mind.

2. Every healthy choice I make brings me closer to

my goals.

3. I honor my body with nutritious food and energetic

movement.

4. I enjoy the journey of becoming my healthiest self.

5. I am capable of achieving my fitness goals.

6. I am grateful for my strong and resilient body.

7. I listen to my body and respect its needs.

8. I choose foods that nourish and energize me.

9. I celebrate my progress, no matter how small.

10. I am empowered to create a healthy lifestyle.

11. My body deserves love, care, and respect.

12. I find joy in physical activity and movement.

13. I embrace a balanced lifestyle that includes rest and play.

14. I nourish my body with love and attentiveness.

15. I am strong, capable, and full of vitality.

16. I make time for self-care and prioritize my health.

17. I am grateful for the energy and vitality of my body.

18. I choose to fuel my body with wholesome ingredients.

19. I am mindful of my eating habits and make conscious choices.

20. I am worth the effort it takes to be healthy.

21. I enjoy cooking nutritious meals that satisfy my body and soul.

22. I have the power to create sustainable, healthy habits.

23. I embrace challenges as opportunities to grow stronger.

24. I am in tune with my body's hunger and fullness signals.

25. I focus on progress, not perfection, on my health journey.

26. I surround myself with supportive and positive influences.

27. I celebrate the small victories along the way.

28. I love to move my body in ways that feel good.

29. I am committed to lifelong learning about health and wellness.

30. I approach exercise as a joyful and rewarding experience.

31. I respect my body's limits and work within them.

32. I cultivate a mindset of health and well-being.

33. I am worthy of good health and happiness.

34. I cherish the connection between my mind and body.

35. I invite healing and wellness into my life.

36. I nourish my mind with positive thoughts and affirmations.

37. I am capable of making lasting lifestyle changes.

38. I prioritize hydration and drink plenty of water daily.

39. I approach each meal with gratitude.

40. I embrace a variety of foods that support my health.

41. I am resilient and can adapt to new challenges.

42. I practice gratitude for my body and its capabilities.

43. I am an inspiration to myself and others on this journey.

44. I am committed to reducing stress through healthy habits.

45. I take time to relax and recharge for my overall well-being.

46. I trust my intuition when it comes to my health choices.

47. I surround myself with healthy, motivating environments.

48. I am focused on creating a balanced and fulfilling life.

49. I appreciate the journey of self-discovery in my health.

50. I engage in physical activities that bring me joy and fulfillment.

51. I nourish my body with colorful, fresh, whole foods.

52. I acknowledge and honor my body's progress and changes.

53. I am committed to my mental and emotional well-being.

54. I celebrate my strength and endurance.

55. I listen to my body's needs and respond with kindness.

56. I embrace positive thoughts and release negativity about my body.

57. I see challenges as opportunities to become healthier.

58. I prioritize sleep and rest as essential components of wellness.

59. I create space in my life for health and vitality.

60. I am proactive in seeking information about nutrition and fitness.

61. I am patient with myself as I work toward my goals.

62. I cultivate joy and gratitude in every step of my journey.

63. I enjoy the process of cooking and preparing my meals.

64. I am thankful for the ability to move and be active.

65. I choose to see my body as a source of strength and beauty.

66. I practice self-love and acceptance every day.

67. I am in control of my health and lifestyle choices.

68. I am inspired by my own commitment to wellness.

69. I focus on the positive changes I am making in my life.

70. I find motivation in the progress I've already made.

71. I prioritize making time for physical activity every day.

72. My inner-strength guides me toward better health decisions.

73. I am grateful for the delicious and nourishing foods I enjoy.

74. I acknowledge and honor my emotional health as well.

75. I love my body for all that it does for me.

76. I practice moderation and balance in my diet.

77. I am a positive example of health and fitness to those around me.

78. I take pride in each step I take towards my well-being.

79. I am proud of my commitment to living a healthier life.

80. I choose to embrace a holistic approach to my health.

81. I am learning to enjoy the journey towards a healthier lifestyle.

82. I am grateful for the challenges that help me grow stronger.

83. I engage in activities that promote my overall well-being.

84. I am resilient in the face of setbacks and continue to move forward.

85. I find pleasure in exploring new healthy recipes and foods.

86. I nourish my body with wholesome, organic choices.

87. I feel energized after every workout and physical activity.

88. I am at peace with my body and appreciate its unique journey.

89. I cultivate healthy relationships that support my well-being.

90. I focus on progress and celebrate my evolving health journey.

91. I practice awareness in my eating habits and daily activities.

92. I am confident in my ability to make healthy choices.

93. I engage in self-reflection to understand my health needs better.

94. I take small, consistent steps toward my health goals.

95. I enjoy the benefits of a balanced and nutritious diet.

96. I am motivated by the positive changes I see in my life.

97. I invite peace and balance into my daily routine.

98. I prioritize regular exercise and make it a joyful experience.

99. I am worthy of a healthy, vibrant, and fulfilling life.

100. I embrace my journey to well-being with love and patience.

# 4

## Nurturing Positive Relationships.

Affectionate affirmations that encourage self-love and the building of meaningful connections with others.

# Chapter 4

## Nurturing Positive Relationships..

Affectionate affirmations that encourage self-love and the building of meaningful connections with others.

Human connection is one of the most fundamental aspects of our lives; it brings joy, support, and a sense of belonging. Nurturing positive relationships not only enriches our personal experiences but also contributes significantly to our emotional and mental well-being. The connections we cultivate with others shape our lives and influence our journey toward growth, happiness, and fulfillment.

In this chapter, you will find affectionate affirmations designed to encourage self-love and foster meaningful connections with those around you. These positive statements serve as gentle reminders to value yourself and to appreciate the unique qualities that you bring to your relationships. When you nurture self-acceptance and self-love, you create a strong foundation for building healthy and empowering connections with others.

Affirmations are powerful tools that help shift our mindset, encouraging us to approach relationships with an open heart and a spirit of generosity. By practicing these affirmations, you will reinforce the importance of empathy, kindness, and understanding in your interactions. As you cultivate a loving relationship with yourself, you naturally attract positive and nurturing relationships with others.

Moreover, the affirmations in this chapter invite you to reflect on the qualities you seek in your connections and encourage you to express gratitude for the relationships that enrich your life. They remind you that building meaningful connections requires effort, patience, and vulnerability, but the rewards of deep, satisfying relationships are immeasurable.

As you engage with these affirmations, take the time to envision the vibrant, supportive relationships you wish to create in your life. Allow them to inspire you to express love and appreciation toward yourself and those around you. Let's embark on this journey of nurturing positive relationships together, fostering connections that uplift, inspire, and nourish our souls!

1. I am worthy of love and respect from others.

2. I attract healthy and supportive relationships into

my life.

3. I communicate openly and honestly with those I

care about.

4. I am surrounded by people who uplift and inspire me.

5. I love and accept myself unconditionally.

6. I value my relationships and nurture them with care.

7. I forgive myself and others, releasing negativity.

8. I am open to giving and receiving love in all forms.

9. I celebrate the unique qualities of my friends and loved ones.

10. I choose to surround myself with positive influences.

11. I am a compassionate friend and listener.

12. I express my feelings honestly and respectfully.

13. I appreciate the people in my life who support me.

14. I am worthy of deep, meaningful connections.

15. I am authentic in my relationships and embrace vulnerability.

16. I attract nurturing and loving relationships.

17. I create healthy boundaries that honor my needs.

18. I invest time and energy in the relationships that matter most.

19. I express gratitude for the love I receive from others.

20. I am open to learning and growing through my relationships.

21. I celebrate the joy of companionship and connection.

22. I practice empathy and understanding in my interactions.

23. I honor my feelings and the feelings of others.

24. I choose to forgive and move forward in my relationships.

25. I create a safe space for open communication.

26. I attract people who appreciate and value me.

27. I am deserving of kindness and compassion from others.

28. I express love and appreciation freely and regularly.

29. I nourish my relationships with trust and honesty.

30. I seek to understand others and be understood in return.

31. I create moments of joy and connection with loved ones.

32. I forgive past hurts and embrace the present with love.

33. I celebrate the diversity of relationships in my life.

34. I am patient and understanding with myself and others.

35. I communicate my needs and desires clearly.

36. I nurture my friendships with love and attention.

37. I am a source of positivity and encouragement in my relationships.

38. I embrace vulnerability as a pathway to deeper connections.

39. I respond to conflicts with love and compassion.

40. I choose relationships that bring me happiness and fulfillment.

41. I am open to new friendships and connections.

42. I honor the relationships that lift me higher.

43. I practice active listening and show genuine interest in others.

44. I attract people who align with my values and goals.

45. I am grateful for the lessons learned from my relationships.

46. I am committed to personal growth within my connections.

47. I make an effort to connect with loved ones regularly.

48. I express my affection openly and sincerely.

49. I am open-hearted and invite love into my life.

50. I appreciate and celebrate the good qualities in others.

51. I surround myself with people who challenge and inspire me.

52. I prioritize quality time with the people I care about.

53. I contribute positivity and joy to my relationships.

54. I communicate with kindness and respect.

55. I bring joy and laughter to my interactions with others.

56. I am worthy of love and belonging in my relationships.

57. I embrace the uniqueness of each person in my life.

58. I value and respect my own needs and boundaries.

59. I release toxic relationships that no longer serve me.

60. I nurture my family bonds with love and understanding.

61. I practice gratitude for the connections I have.

62. I affirm love and compassion in my relationships daily.

63. I build bridges of understanding and compassion.

64. I am drawn to people who uplift and empower me.

65. I celebrate the moments of connection in everyday life.

66. I honor my intuition in choosing my relationships.

67. I am a beacon of love and positivity for my friends.

68. I create time for meaningful conversations with loved ones.

69. I seek connections that resonate with my authentic self.

70. I spread love and kindness to everyone I meet.

71. I can be myself with the people I love.

72. I love myself deeply, which allows me to love others fully.

73. I trust that the right people will come into my life.

74. I nurture my relationships with acts of kindness and love.

75. I foster an environment of support and encouragement.

76. I honor the commitments I make to my loved ones.

77. I create lasting memories with people I cherish.

78. I choose to be present and engaged in my relationships.

79. I am a loving and supportive partner/friend/family member.

80. I listen to my heart and trust my feelings in relationships.

81. I am grateful for the beautiful connections in my life.

82. I embrace change and growth in my relationships.

83. I am constantly growing in my ability to love and connect with others.

84. I let go of past grievances and focus on building a brighter future.

85. I am committed to creating a loving and harmonious home environment.

86. I foster a mindset of abundance in my relationships.

87. I appreciate the support and encouragement I receive from others.

88. I choose to see the best in the people around me.

89. I cultivate trust and loyalty in my friendships.

90. I express my feelings with honesty and integrity.

91. I create opportunities for deep and meaningful conversations.

92. I welcome love and connection into every aspect of my life.

93. I celebrate the unique gifts and talents of my loved ones.

94. I am attuned to the needs and emotions of those I care about.

95. I build strong connections based on mutual respect and understanding.

96. I actively participate in nurturing my relationships with love.

97. I embrace the joy that comes from giving and receiving affection.

98. I allow love to guide my interactions and decisions.

99. I honor and cherish the special bonds I share with others.

100. I believe in my ability to create and sustain positive relationships.

# 5

## Achieving Abundance and Success.

Focus on affirmations that align with attracting financial success and opportunities for growth.

# Chapter 5

## Achieving Abundance and Success.

Focus on affirmations that align with attracting financial success and opportunities for growth.

The pursuit of abundance and success is a fundamental aspect of the human experience, driving us to seek opportunities that enrich our lives and the lives of those we love. However, achieving true abundance is not solely about accumulating wealth; it encompasses a mindset that embraces growth, prosperity, and fulfillment in every aspect of life. Cultivating a wealth-conscious attitude opens the door to endless possibilities and empowers you to attract the success you desire.

In this chapter, you will find powerful affirmations designed to align your thoughts and beliefs with abundance and success. These affirmations serve as catalysts for transforming your mindset, encouraging you to recognize and embrace the opportunities that surround you. By adopting a positive outlook on your financial and personal growth, you empower yourself to break through limiting beliefs that may have held you back.

Affirmations foster a sense of confidence and self-worth, reminding you that you are deserving of success, prosperity, and happiness. As you integrate these affirmations into your daily routine, you will cultivate a habit of thinking abundantly, enabling you to seize opportunities and make empowered decisions that align with your goals.

Moreover, these affirmations will inspire you to adopt a growth-focused mindset, encouraging you to view challenges as stepping stones rather than barriers. They remind you that every experience—whether perceived as a success or a setback—provides valuable lessons that contribute to your overall journey toward abundance.

As you engage with these affirmations, take time to visualize your goals and the life you wish to create. Allow them to inspire a proactive approach towards achieving your dreams, leading you to recognize the abundance that is already present in your life and what you can create in the future. Together, let's embark on this journey of attracting financial success and opportunities for growth, embracing the abundant possibilities that await you!

1. I am worthy of abundance and success in my life.

2. I attract wealth and opportunities effortlessly.

3. I am open to receiving all the abundance the

universe offers.

4. I create my own financial success through hard work and determination.

5. My mindset is focused on abundance and prosperity.

6. I embrace opportunities that come my way with gratitude.

7. I am capable of achieving my financial goals.

8. I am surrounded by endless possibilities for success.

9. I deserve to live a life of abundance and fulfillment.

10. I attract positive, like-minded people into my life.

11. I make wise financial decisions that support my dreams.

12. I am grateful for the abundance that flows into my life.

13. I believe in my ability to manifest financial success.

14. I am a magnet for wealth and prosperity.

15. I release limiting beliefs about money and success.

16. I am confident in my abilities to create financial freedom.

17. I am constantly growing and evolving on my path to success.

18. I take inspired action toward my goals every day.

19. I celebrate my progress and the abundance it brings.

20. I attract opportunities that align with my passions and purpose.

21. I am worthy of a life filled with prosperity and joy.

22. I communicate openly about my financial goals.

23. I focus on solutions, not problems, in my financial journey.

24. I trust that the universe supports my desires for abundance.

25. I am deserving of all the riches life has to offer.

26. I visualize my financial success and take steps to achieve it.

27. I am resilient and adaptable in the face of challenges.

28. I am skilled at finding creative solutions to financial challenges.

29. I attract success and prosperity in my career.

30. My financial knowledge and skills are continuously improving.

31. I release fear and embrace confidence in my financial decisions.

32. I am empowered to create the life I desire.

33. I actively seek out new opportunities for growth.

34. I am open to receiving financial blessings from unexpected sources.

35. I celebrate the financial successes of others as my own.

36. I set achievable goals that lead to abundance and success.

37. I am in control of my financial destiny.

38. I am open to learning from both successes and failures.

39. I attract lucrative opportunities that enhance my life.

40. I am deserving of a prosperous and abundant lifestyle.

41. I surround myself with positive influences that uplift my financial journey.

42. I am confident in my ability to create wealth.

43. I learn and grow from every financial experience.

44. I am patient and persistent in pursuing my goals.

45. I align my actions with my vision of success.

46. I visualize myself living a life of abundance every day.

47. I believe in the infinite possibilities for my financial future.

48. I attract resources and support that help me achieve my goals.

49. I am constantly discovering new ways to create abundance.

50. I embrace financial independence and freedom.

51. I trust myself to make sound investment decisions.

52. I am grateful for the financial security I am building.

53. I welcome abundance into my life with open arms.

54. I am in tune with my financial well-being and happiness.

55. I create value in everything I do, which brings me success.

56. I release old patterns that no longer serve my financial goals.

57. I am a successful creator of my own destiny.

58. I attract prosperity through my positive mindset.

59. I am motivated by my passion and purpose in life.

60. I recognize and embrace my financial potential.

61. I am capable of achieving everything I desire.

62. I welcome growth and transformation in my financial journey.

63. I celebrate my financial victories, no matter how small.

64. I choose to thrive financially and personally.

65. I am worthy of receiving financial rewards for my efforts.

66. I cultivate an attitude of gratitude that attracts more abundance.

67. I am focused on my goals and take consistent action toward them.

68. I embrace the journey to financial freedom with enthusiasm.

69. I invest in myself and my personal development.

70. I provide valuable services that are rewarded financially.

71. I trust the path I am on and the opportunities it presents.

72. I am flexible and adapt my strategies as needed for success.

73. I actively create a career that brings me joy and fulfillment.

74. I am comfortable discussing money and financial matters.

75. I honor my finances and treat money with respect.

76. I am persistent and dedicated to achieving my financial goals.

77. I attract abundance and success with my positive energy.

78. I am open to new paths leading to wealth and opportunity.

79. I am worthy of success and embrace it fully.

80. I nurture my financial growth through positive habits.

81. I am aligned with the energy of abundance and success in every aspect of my life.

82. I take time to celebrate my financial milestones, big and small.

83. I am capable of turning my dreams into reality.

84. I am always attracting greater wealth and opportunities.

85. I cultivate a mindset that fosters financial growth and achievement.

86. I am grateful for the lessons that come from every financial experience.

87. I focus on abundance rather than scarcity in my thoughts.

88. I create a life filled with richness in experiences and finances.

89. I attract mentors and teachers who support my financial journey.

90. I am deserving of living a life of luxury and comfort.

91. I awaken each day ready to take steps toward abundance.

92. I reflect on my successes and learn from my challenges.

93. I am a powerful creator of my financial reality.

94. I trust that every setback is a setup for a comeback.

95. I visualize my success daily and act in alignment with it.

96. I am committed to lifelong growth and improvement.

97. I welcome change as an opportunity for financial advancement.

98. I give and receive generously, creating cycles of abundance.

99. I am thankful for the financial blessings in my life.

100. I shine brightly as I attract the success that is meant for me.

# 6

## Cultivating a Mindset of Resilience.

Affirmations that help develop perseverance, encouraging you to overcome obstacles and setbacks.

# Chapter 6

## Cultivating a Mindset of Resilience.

Affirmations that help develop perseverance, encouraging you to overcome obstacles and setbacks.

Life is a journey filled with ups and downs, and developing a resilient mindset is essential for navigating its inevitable challenges. Resilience is not about avoiding adversity; rather, it is the ability to bounce back and grow stronger from setbacks, embracing every experience as an opportunity for learning and personal development. Cultivating a mindset of resilience empowers us to face obstacles with confidence and determination, transforming adversity into stepping stones toward our goals.

In this chapter, you will find affirmations specifically designed to help you develop perseverance and strengthen your ability to overcome challenges. These positive statements serve as powerful reminders that you hold the capacity to weather storms and emerge even more capable than before. By practicing these affirmations regularly, you will reinforce your belief in your resilience and ability to navigate life's complexities.

The affirmations in this chapter encourage a shift in perspective, allowing you to view challenges as opportunities for growth rather than as insurmountable barriers. This mindset fosters a greater sense of empowerment and confidence in your ability to confront difficulties. When you affirm your strengths and resilience, you create a positive feedback loop; each success builds upon the last, reinforcing your ability to tackle future challenges.

Moreover, embracing resilience allows you to cultivate emotional intelligence, enabling you to cope with stress and uncertainty more effectively. You will find that as you develop a resilient mindset, you become better equipped to manage change, adapt to unforeseen circumstances, and maintain a sense of hope even in trying times.

As you engage with these affirmations, take a moment to reflect on the challenges you have faced and how they have shaped you. Allow the strength of your past experiences to inspire you as you cultivate the resilience needed to tackle whatever lies ahead. Let's embark on this transformative journey together, fostering a mindset of resilience that empowers you to thrive in all aspects of life!

1. I am resilient and capable of overcoming any

challenge.

2. I embrace setbacks as opportunities for growth and

learning.

3. I possess the strength to rise above difficulties.

4. I am committed to pushing through and persisting.

5. I trust in my ability to navigate life's obstacles.

6. I welcome challenges as a chance to develop my character.

7. I learn valuable lessons from my experiences.

8. I am stronger than my fears and doubts.

9. I celebrate my progress, no matter how small.

10. I am determined to keep moving forward, no matter what.

11. I focus on solutions rather than problems.

12. I have the courage to face adversity head-on.

13. I believe in my ability to adapt and thrive.

14. I am grateful for the lessons that my challenges teach me.

15. I can transform setbacks into valuable opportunities.

16. I maintain a positive outlook, even during tough times.

17. I am persistent in pursuing my goals despite obstacles.

18. I cultivate a mindset of flexibility and resilience.

19. I trust that I can handle whatever comes my way.

20. I am not defined by my struggles; I am defined by how I respond to them.

21. I choose to rise after every fall and keep going.

22. I embrace discomfort as a part of my growth journey.

23. I am patient with myself as I work through challenges.

24. I focus on my strengths and use them to overcome difficulties.

25. I learn and grow stronger from every experience.

26. I surround myself with supportive people who uplift me.

27. I am capable of turning adversity into strength.

28. I release the need for perfection and embrace progress.

29. I celebrate my ability to keep going when things get tough.

30. I trust my resilience to carry me through hard times.

31. I am committed to my personal and emotional growth.

32. I have the power to transform obstacles into stepping stones.

33. I appreciate the strength that comes from overcoming challenges.

34. I keep my mind open to new possibilities and solutions.

35. I take one step at a time, trusting the process.

36. I acknowledge my feelings and allow myself to heal.

37. I am equipped to handle change and uncertainty.

38. I face challenges with confidence and courage.

39. I can adapt to any situation that comes my way.

40. I choose to learn from my mistakes and move forward.

41. I embrace resilience as a part of my character.

42. I am on a journey of growth and self-discovery.

43. I remain hopeful and optimistic about the future.

44. I am capable of overcoming any limitation I perceive.

45. I trust that every challenge I face serves a greater purpose.

46. I am empowered by the knowledge that I can persevere.

47. I take time to reflect on my progress and solutions.

48. I embrace each setback as a valuable part of my journey.

49. I am skilled at finding strength in adversity.

50. I am a survivor and thrive in the face of challenges.

51. I keep my heart open to hope and positive change.

52. I reinforce my resilience through self-compassion.

53. I am determined to keep striving, regardless of difficulties.

54. I approach challenges with confidence and positivity.

55. I draw upon my inner strength to power through tough times.

56. I invest in my well-being and emotional health.

57. I trust in my ability to overcome obstacles.

58. I am always moving forward, no matter the pace.

59. I appreciate the journey and the lessons learned along the way.

60. I cultivate a mindset of grit and determination.

61. I believe in myself, even when times are tough.

62. I acknowledge my progress and honor my efforts.

63. I find creative solutions to overcome challenges.

64. I am open to change and growth in every area of my life.

65. I choose to focus on what I can control.

66. I am emotionally resilient and capable of bouncing back.

67. I trust the process and have faith in my journey.

68. I invite resilience into my life and let it guide me.

69. I acknowledge my strength in facing adversity every day.

70. I can handle anything life throws my way.

71. I draw strength from my past experiences to face the future.

72. I cultivate an unwavering belief in my abilities.

73. I embrace my vulnerabilities as a path to strength.

74. I am willing to step outside of my comfort zone.

75. I use my challenges as fuel for personal growth.

76. I take inspiration from others who have overcome obstacles.

77. I am determined to chase my dreams, no matter the hurdles.

78. I find joy in the process of overcoming difficulties.

79. I take responsibility for my growth and choices.

80. I remain steadfast in my commitment to my goals.

81. I approach each day with renewed strength and determination.

82. I embrace uncertainty as a natural part of life's journey.

83. I have the courage to confront my fears and move forward.

84. I trust that every challenge strengthens my character.

85. I cultivate gratitude for the resilience I possess.

86. I allow myself to feel emotions while remaining focused on solutions.

87. I am continuously evolving and adapting to my circumstances.

88. I rely on my inner wisdom to guide me through tough times.

89. I am a strong and capable problem-solver.

90. I celebrate my ability to bounce back from setbacks.

91. I approach obstacles as opportunities for creative growth.

92. I have faith in my ability to overcome any situation.

93. I am open to seeking help and support when needed.

94. I develop my resilience through self-reflection.

95. I confidently navigate life's ups and downs.

96. I embrace each challenge as a chance to become better.

97. I remind myself of my past successes to fuel my present efforts.

98. I am grateful for my journey and the strength it builds within me.

99. I surround myself with positivity and encouragement.

100. I align my thoughts and actions with a resilient mindset.

# 7

## Embracing Change and New Beginnings.

Positive words that inspire embracing transitions and stepping out of comfort zones.

# Chapter 7

# Embracing Change and New Beginnings.

Positive words that inspire embracing transitions and stepping out of comfort zones.

Change is an inherent part of life, and while it can often feel daunting, it also presents us with incredible opportunities for growth and transformation. Embracing change means stepping into the unknown with courage and an open heart, allowing us to discover new possibilities and redefine our paths. New beginnings can invigorate our lives, fueling personal development and revitalizing our aspirations.

In this chapter, you will find positive affirmations designed to inspire you to embrace transitions and step out of your comfort zone. These affirmations serve as powerful tools to help shift your mindset, encouraging you to view change as an opportunity rather than a threat. By allowing these words to resonate with you, you create a fertile ground for personal growth and self-discovery.

Embracing change requires a willingness to let go of the familiar and to trust in the unfolding of your journey. With every transition, we are given the chance to learn more about ourselves, adapt to new circumstances, and cultivate resilience. Each affirmation in this chapter encourages you to accept the beauty of impermanence and to find strength in your ability to adapt.

Moreover, stepping out of your comfort zone can be transformative; it invites new experiences, perspectives, and connections into your life. As you embrace change, you may discover hidden talents, strengthen your self-confidence, and develop a deeper understanding of your core values and desires.

As you engage with these affirmations, take time to reflect on your current situation and the new beginnings you desire. Allow these inspiring words to empower you to take the necessary steps toward embracing change and cultivating a life filled with exploration and adventure. Let's embark on this exciting journey together, welcoming change as an essential part of our personal evolution and a gateway to new horizons!

1. I welcome change as a natural part of life's journey.

2. I am excited about the new opportunities that change brings.

3. I embrace transitions with an open heart and mind.

4. I have the courage to step out of my comfort zone.

5. I trust that change leads me to greater growth and fulfillment.

6. I see challenges as a chance to learn and evolve.

7. I am open to new experiences and perspectives.

8. I embrace every new beginning with enthusiasm.

9. I find strength in my ability to adapt to change.

10. I release fear and embrace the possibilities of the unknown.

11. I am the architect of my own transformation.

12. I trust the journey and have faith in my path.

13. I celebrate my progress and my willingness to change.

14. I am resilient and fully capable of navigating transitions.

15. I am excited to see what the future holds for me.

16. I attract positive energy through embracing change.

17. I can adapt and thrive in new environments.

18. I am grateful for the lessons that change brings me.

19. I release old patterns that no longer serve my growth.

20. I choose to view change as an opportunity for renewal.

21. I am open to stepping into the unknown with confidence.

22. I cultivate a mindset that welcomes new beginnings.

23. I embrace the discomfort of growth as a sign of progress.

24. I am constantly evolving into the best version of myself.

25. I trust that every ending opens the door to new beginnings.

26. I am excited to explore new possibilities in my life.

27. I embrace change with enthusiasm and curiosity.

28. I find comfort in the knowledge that change is a part of life.

29. I release resistance and embrace the flow of life.

30. I am confident in my ability to navigate new situations.

31. I recognize that change can lead to incredible opportunities.

32. I am grateful for the fresh perspectives that change brings.

33. I am open to discovering new strengths within myself.

34. I embrace uncertainty as a chance for growth and exploration.

35. I am capable of transforming challenges into strengths.

36. I celebrate my courage to try new things.

37. I am excited to expand my horizons through change.

38. I trust my intuition to guide me through transitions.

39. I am confident in my ability to adapt and thrive.

40. I see change as an invitation to new adventures.

41. I embrace flexibility as an important aspect of my growth.

42. I am open to receiving the abundance that change can bring.

43. I welcome fresh starts and new experiences with joy.

44. I am in tune with the rhythm of life's changes.

45. I trust that every step I take leads me closer to my dreams.

46. I celebrate my ability to embrace the unfamiliar.

47. I am proactive in seeking positive change in my life.

48. I allow myself to feel excited about new opportunities.

49. I am limitless in my potential to create change.

50. I embrace new relationships and connections with enthusiasm.

51. I find joy in the possibilities that come with change.

52. I release fears and doubts as I embark on new adventures.

53. I am grateful for every beginning, no matter how small.

54. I cultivate a spirit of curiosity and exploration in my life.

55. I learn and grow from each new experience I encounter.

56. I welcome the challenges that come with change as opportunities.

57. I trust that I am always becoming who I am meant to be.

58. I embrace my journey of self-discovery through change.

59. I reaffirm my commitment to living a life of growth and exploration.

60. I am willing to take risks to achieve my goals.

61. I find strength in every transition I face.

62. I am excited to leave behind what no longer serves me.

63. I recognize that change can lead to profound transformation.

64. I approach new beginnings with a sense of adventure.

65. I am on a path of continuous growth and evolution.

66. I celebrate the opportunities that come with change.

67. I am confident in my ability to shape my own destiny.

68. I embrace changes in my life with positivity and optimism.

69. I trust the timing of my life and the changes that come.

70. I find peace in the unknown and the unexpected.

71. I celebrate the new beginnings that are unfolding for me.

72. I am resilient in the face of change and uncertainty.

73. I am open to receiving all the good that change brings my way.

74. I welcome growth with open arms and an open heart.

75. I choose to see change as a stepping stone to success.

76. I trust that my journey is unfolding perfectly.

77. I am grateful for the opportunities to reinvent myself.

78. I am grateful for the strength I gain from stepping outside my comfort zone.

79. I embrace change as a catalyst for positive transformation.

80. I am willing to let go of the past to embrace new beginnings.

81. I trust that every step I take forward is aligned with my purpose.

82. I approach new adventures with confidence and excitement.

83. I am open to the possibilities that change can bring into my life.

84. I find joy in exploring new paths and opportunities.

85. I am grateful for the wisdom that comes from navigating change.

86. I let go of fear and embrace the excitement of the unknown.

87. I am a pioneer in creating my own future.

88. I trust my ability to find my way through transitions.

89. I take inspired action to create the life I desire.

90. I am open to change as a means of achieving my dreams.

91. I recognize that every ending is a new beginning waiting to unfold.

92. I find strength in my adaptability and resilience.

93. I cultivate a positive attitude toward new experiences.

94. I celebrate the journey of change as much as the destination.

95. I am open to receiving support as I navigate new beginnings.

96. I embrace uncertainty as a chance to grow and learn.

97. I am excited to see how change enhances my life.

98. I cultivate inner peace as I embrace life's transitions.

99. I believe that every challenge facilitates my growth.

100. I am on a journey of self-discovery and empowerment.

# 8

## Fostering Creativity and Inspiration.

Affirmations to unlock creativity and encourage personal expression, helping you find inspiration in your daily life.

# Chapter 8

## Fostering Creativity and Inspiration.

Affirmations to unlock creativity and encourage personal expression, helping you find inspiration in your daily life.

Creativity is a vital force that enriches our lives, enabling us to express ourselves, solve problems, and explore the world around us in new and innovative ways. It is not limited to artistic pursuits; rather, it encompasses a mindset that encourages imaginative thinking and personal expression in all areas of life. By fostering our creativity, we unlock the potential for deeper connections with ourselves and others, as well as the ability to approach challenges with fresh perspectives.

In this chapter, you will discover affirmations designed to unlock your creativity and inspire personal expression. These affirmations serve as gentle reminders of your innate creative potential and encourage you to explore the unique gifts you possess. By incorporating these positive statements into your routine, you create an environment where creativity can thrive, allowing you to break free from self-imposed limitations and embrace your innovative spirit.

The affirmations in this chapter encourage you to view the world through a lens of curiosity and imagination, inviting inspiration to flow into your daily life. By embracing the idea that creativity exists within everyone, you empower yourself to express your thoughts and feelings authentically, whether through art, writing, problem-solving, or any other outlet that resonates with you.

Furthermore, fostering creativity opens the door to personal growth and deeper self-awareness. As you engage with your creative side, you may uncover new passions, discover untapped talents, and develop a more profound understanding of your emotions and experiences. This process not only enhances your creativity but also enriches your overall life experience.

As you explore these affirmations, take time to reflect on what creativity means to you and how it manifests in your life. Allow these words to inspire and motivate you to embrace your unique expressions and find inspiration in everyday moments. Let's embark on this journey of creativity and inspiration together, celebrating the boundless possibilities that arise when we open ourselves to our creative potential!

1. I am a limitless source of creativity and inspiration.

2. I embrace my unique talents and express them freely.

3. My creativity flows effortlessly and abundantly.

4. I create space in my life for inspiration to flourish.

5. I am open to new ideas and perspectives.

6. I trust my intuition to guide my creative journey.

7. I find beauty and inspiration in the world around me.

8. I allow myself to explore and experiment without fear.

9. My imagination knows no bounds, and I celebrate that.

10. I nurture my creative spirit every day.

11. I am worthy of expressing my creative ideas freely.

12. I release self-doubt and embrace my creative potential.

13. I find inspiration in everyday experiences and interactions.

14. I am excited to discover new ways to express myself.

15. My creative energy is vibrant and ever-present.

16. I welcome challenges as opportunities for creative growth.

17. I am inspired by the art and creativity of others.

18. I cultivate a playful attitude towards creativity.

19. My ideas flow freely, and I embrace them wholeheartedly.

20. I am open to receiving inspiration from all around me.

21. I view the creative process as a joyful journey.

22. I trust that my creativity will lead me to new discoveries.

23. I am grateful for the moments of inspiration that come to me.

24. I express myself authentically through my creativity.

25. I find inspiration in nature and the beauty of the world.

26. I take time to nurture my creative passions.

27. I am curious and eager to learn new things.

28. I celebrate my creative wins, big and small.

29. I embrace imperfection as a part of the creative process.

30. My creativity is unique, and I honor it.

31. I trust that ideas will come to me when I need them.

32. I draw inspiration from my life experiences.

33. I am dedicated to developing my creative skills.

34. I seek out new experiences to fuel my creativity.

35. I allow myself the freedom to create without judgment.

36. I can find creativity in the simplest of things.

37. I am inspired by the world around me every day.

38. I trust that my creativity is valuable and important.

39. I create a supportive environment for my creativity to thrive.

40. I embrace change as a source of inspiration and innovation.

41. I allow my imagination to take me on new adventures.

42. I engage in creative activities that bring me joy.

43. I appreciate my unique perspective and insights.

44. I inspire others through my own creative expression.

45. I find strength in vulnerability when sharing my art.

46. I am open to collaborating with others on creative projects.

47. I listen to my inner voice and allow it to guide me.

48. I take risks in my creativity and learn from them.

49. I prioritize time for my creative pursuits each day.

50. I am surrounded by endless sources of inspiration.

51. My creativity flows abundantly when I trust myself.

52. I allow my thoughts and feelings to inform my creative work.

53. I celebrate the diversity of creativity in myself and others.

54. I keep an open mind to new creative possibilities.

55. I am willing to step outside my comfort zone in my art.

56. I engage in introspection to connect with my creativity.

57. I appreciate the process of creating as much as the final result.

58. I show compassion to myself during my creative journey.

59. I am passionate about exploring new forms of expression.

60. I invite magic and serendipity into my creative process.

61. I am willing to be a beginner and learn as I go.

62. I trust that creativity can be found in the mundane.

63. I allow myself to dream big and pursue my passions.

64. I celebrate my individuality and express it confidently.

65. I am not afraid to share my ideas and creations with the world.

66. I take inspiration from my dreams and daydreams.

67. I create daily rituals that encourage my creative flow.

68. I am in tune with my creative flow and honor it.

69. I find joy in the exploration of my artistic interests.

70. I appreciate the journey of self-discovery through creativity.

71. I surround myself with supportive and like-minded individuals.

72. I recognize the importance of rest in nurturing creativity.

73. I allow my creativity to evolve and change over time.

74. I seek inspiration in books, art, and nature.

75. I am flexible and adaptive in my creative pursuits.

76. I express my emotions through my creative outlets.

77. I celebrate the connections made through creative collaboration.

78. I practice gratitude for my creative gifts and talents.

79. I enjoy the freedom that comes with creative expression.

80. I am a creative being, and my imagination knows no bounds.

81. I am continuously inspired by the beauty and diversity of life.

82. I embrace the unknown as a canvas for my creativity.

83. I allow myself to dream without limits and explore my ideas.

84. I find inspiration in the stories and experiences of others.

85. I honor my creative process and its unique rhythms.

86. I am willing to experiment and play with my creative expressions.

87. I seek out new environments that spark my creativity.

88. I embrace spontaneity as a source of inspiration.

89. I am grounded in the present while exploring creative possibilities.

90. I visualize my creative projects and bring them to life.

91. I find peace in the act of creation and self-expression.

92. I create with love, passion, and a sense of purpose.

93. I celebrate and acknowledge my creative milestones.

94. I cultivate a curious mindset that fuels my creativity.

95. I trust my instincts and allow them to guide my creative choices.

96. I am inspired by the challenges I face and transform them into art.

97. I see failures as setups for my greater creative growth.

98. I am open to feedback and use it to enhance my creativity.

99. I embrace rituals that inspire my creativity every day.

100. I am grateful for the opportunity to share my creativity with the world.

# 9

## Nurturing Self-Acceptance and Love.

Positive affirmations that reinforce the importance of loving oneself and embracing individuality.

# Chapter 9

## Nurturing Self-Acceptance and Love.

Positive affirmations that reinforce the importance of loving oneself and embracing individuality.

In a world that often emphasizes comparison and external validation, nurturing self-acceptance and love is essential for achieving emotional well-being and personal fulfillment. Embracing who we are—flaws, strengths, and everything in between—allows us to cultivate a profound sense of worthiness and authenticity. When we honor our individuality, we unlock the door to self-discovery and connectedness, enabling us to engage more fully with ourselves and those around us.

In this chapter, you will find a collection of positive affirmations designed to reinforce the importance of loving yourself and embracing your unique qualities. These affirmations serve as powerful allies in your journey toward self-acceptance, helping to silence the critical inner voice that may hinder your growth. By practicing these affirmations regularly, you create a nurturing environment where self-love can flourish.

The affirmations in this chapter encourage you to look within and recognize your inherent value. They remind you that acceptance is not about conforming to societal standards; instead, it is about celebrating your individuality and honoring your unique path. By embracing your true self, you empower yourself to live authentically and joyfully.

Furthermore, nurturing self-acceptance fosters resilience, allowing you to navigate life's challenges with compassion for yourself. As you cultivate love within, you become better equipped to form meaningful connections with others, creating an inclusive environment where everyone feels valued and respected.

As you engage with these affirmations, take a moment to reflect on your strengths and the qualities that make you who you are. Allow these words to inspire a deeper appreciation for yourself and your journey, leading you to embrace and love the person you are becoming. Let's embark on this transformative journey of self-acceptance and love together, celebrating the beauty of our individuality!

1. I am worthy of love and acceptance just as I am.

2. I honor my unique journey and celebrate my

individuality.

3. I embrace my flaws as part of what makes me

beautiful.

4. I am enough, exactly as I am in this moment.

5. I choose to love myself unconditionally.

6. I acknowledge my strengths and celebrate my achievements.

7. I am grateful for my body and all it does for me.

8. I treat myself with kindness and compassion.

9. I am deserving of all the good things life has to offer.

10. I accept my feelings and allow myself to experience them fully.

11. I embrace my uniqueness and let my true self shine.

12. I am proud of who I am and who I am becoming.

13. I nurture my mind, body, and soul with love and care.

14. I forgive myself for past mistakes and learn from them.

15. I am a work in progress, and I enjoy the journey of growth.

16. I surround myself with positivity that uplifts my spirit.

17. I trust my intuition and honor my own opinions.

18. I cultivate a deep sense of self-worth and self-love.

19. I celebrate my individuality and express it freely.

20. I am at peace with my past and excited for my future.

21. I practice self-care and prioritize my well-being.

22. I am resilient and capable of overcoming challenges.

23. I radiate confidence and attract positivity into my life.

24. I am grateful for my unique talents and abilities.

25. I choose to see the beauty in my imperfections.

26. I surround myself with people who appreciate me for who I am.

27. I honor my needs and set healthy boundaries.

28. I am my own best advocate and cheerleader.

29. I embrace change and see it as an opportunity for growth.

30. I deserve to take up space in this world.

31. I am continually becoming a better version of myself.

32. I choose to focus on my accomplishments and progress.

33. I am filled with self-love every day.

34. I accept and embrace all parts of myself.

35. I am worthy of respect and kindness from myself and others.

36. I trust that I am exactly where I need to be in my journey.

37. I am enough, I do enough, and I have enough.

38. I allow my authentic self to shine without fear.

39. I release the need for external validation and trust myself.

40. I acknowledge my growth and celebrate my resilience.

41. I forgive myself and move forward with love.

42. I honor my journey and the lessons I have learned.

43. I embrace my quirks as unique expressions of who I am.

44. I am deserving of love and happiness in my life.

45. I cherish my individuality and contribute it to the world.

46. I breathe in love and exhale self-doubt.

47. I am compassionate towards myself during difficult times.

48. I deserve to be my first priority and focus on my needs.

49. I celebrate my journey and trust the process of life.

50. I contribute positively to the world by being my true self.

51. I am proud of my accomplishments, both big and small.

52. I let go of comparison and embrace my unique path.

53. I am kind to myself in my thoughts and actions.

54. I celebrate my unique perspective and voice.

55. I live with intention and purpose, embracing my authenticity.

56. I practice gratitude for who I am every day.

57. I honor my own journey and recognize its value.

58. I am worthy of love, respect, and kindness from myself.

59. I am constantly evolving and embracing the journey.

60. I forgive myself for being human and allow for growth.

61. I nurture my talents and express them with joy.

62. I affirm my self-worth daily with positive thoughts.

63. I accept my past experiences and celebrate my growth.

64. I fill my mind with thoughts of love and appreciation for myself.

65. I radiate positive energy and attract like-minded individuals.

66. I am perfect in my imperfections and beautifully me.

67. I prioritize my happiness and well-being above all.

68. I embrace challenges as opportunities for growth and learning.

69. I am at peace with my journey and trust in the process.

70. I seek joy in my daily life and celebrate it.

71. I cultivate a deep sense of self-acceptance and confidence.

72. I let love guide my actions towards myself and others.

73. I release negativity and embrace a mindset of positivity.

74. I honor my feelings and allow myself to experience them.

75. I deserve to express my needs and desires openly.

76. I acknowledge my progress and celebrate my achievements.

77. I surround myself with love and positive energy.

78. I trust in my ability to create the life I desire.

79. I affirm my worth and recognize the value I bring to the world.

80. I let go of self-judgment and embrace self-compassion.

81. I create a safe space within myself to grow and learn.

82. I nourish my spirit with love, understanding, and patience.

83. I celebrate my uniqueness, knowing it enriches the world.

84. I accept my past as part of my journey and embrace my future.

85. I am worthy of my dreams and dedicated to pursuing them.

86. I shine brightly, illuminating the path for myself and others.

87. I honor my individuality and let it guide my choices.

88. I am deserving of care, love, and attention from myself.

89. I release the need for approval from others, trusting myself instead.

90. I acknowledge my feelings as valid and worthy of attention.

91. I am responsible for my own happiness and nurture it daily.

92. I affirm that my true self is enough and worthy of love.

93. I embrace every aspect of who I am with love and acceptance.

94. I am empowered by my self-acceptance and inner strength.

95. I let love and acceptance flow effortlessly into my life.

96. I recognize that my uniqueness is a gift to the world.

97. I cherish my journey of self-discovery and personal growth.

98. I take pride in my accomplishments and celebrate my efforts.

99. I embrace my individuality with confidence and grace.

100. I acknowledge that I am a masterpiece in progress.

# 10

## Gratitude and Reflection.

Affirmations that encourage a practice of gratitude, helping you appreciate your journey and achievements.

# Chapter 10

# Gratitude and Reflection.

Affirmations that encourage a practice of gratitude, helping you appreciate your journey and achievements.

Gratitude is a transformative practice that has the power to enrich our lives and shift our perspectives. By focusing on what we are thankful for, we open our hearts and minds to the abundance all around us. Cultivating a sense of gratitude encourages us to appreciate the journey we are on, recognize our achievements, and find joy in even the smallest moments of life. When we engage in reflection, we take the time to acknowledge our experiences and understand their significance, allowing us to grow and evolve.

In this chapter, you will find affirmations designed to inspire a daily practice of gratitude and reflection. These positive statements serve as gentle reminders to focus on the blessings in our lives, reinforcing the importance of appreciating your unique journey and recognizing how far you have come. By incorporating these affirmations into your routine, you create a powerful mindset that fosters positivity and gratitude in everyday life.

The affirmations in this chapter encourage you to acknowledge both the struggles and triumphs that shape your experiences. Each step along your journey contributes to your growth, helping you develop resilience and insight. By reflecting on your achievements and the lessons learned from challenges, you cultivate a deeper appreciation for the person you are becoming.

Moreover, practicing gratitude enhances our overall well-being, promoting feelings of happiness and contentment. When we actively express appreciation for our lives, we invite more positive experiences and opportunities to flow in. Gratitude shifts our focus from what we lack to what we have, creating a cycle of abundance that nourishes our spirit.

As you engage with these affirmations, take the time to reflect on the richness of your experiences and the achievements that bring you joy. Allow these words to inspire a consistent practice of gratitude in your life, helping you to appreciate every moment of your journey. Let's embark on this enriching journey of gratitude and reflection together, celebrating the beauty of our experiences and the abundance in our lives!

1. I am grateful for the abundance in my life.

2. I appreciate the lessons that my journey has taught

me.

3. I celebrate my achievements, both big and small.

4. I find joy in the little things that make life special.

5. I am thankful for the support of my loved ones.

6. I reflect on my experiences with gratitude and understanding.

7. I express appreciation for the opportunities that come my way.

8. I am grateful for my health and well-being.

9. I take time each day to acknowledge my blessings.

10. I embrace a mindset of gratitude, attracting positivity into my life.

11. I honor my accomplishments and the effort it took to achieve them.

12. I appreciate the beauty of nature and the world around me.

13. I am thankful for the strengths I have developed on my journey.

14. I practice gratitude as a way to cultivate happiness.

15. I recognize the support I receive from the universe.

16. I cherish the moments of joy that fill my days.

17. I am grateful for the opportunities to learn and grow.

18. I reflect on my progress and celebrate how far I have come.

19. I find peace in the present moment and express gratitude for it.

20. I connect with my inner self through reflection and appreciation.

21. I appreciate the love and kindness I receive from others.

22. I am thankful for the challenges that have shaped my character.

23. I practice gratitude to create a positive mindset.

24. I celebrate my resilience and ability to overcome obstacles.

25. I honor my journey and the unique experiences that have led me here.

26. I express gratitude for the knowledge I gain through reflection.

27. I am thankful for the growth that comes from adversity.

28. I embrace the power of gratitude to transform my perspective.

29. I appreciate everyday moments that bring me joy.

30. I recognize the abundance of opportunities surrounding me.

31. I am grateful for the connections I share with others.

32. I cherish the lessons that setbacks have taught me.

33. I practice gratitude as a daily ritual.

34. I celebrate the courage it takes to pursue my dreams.

35. I express appreciation for my unique journey in life.

36. I acknowledge the beauty of my experiences, both good and bad.

37. I am thankful for the moments that inspire me to keep going.

38. I reflect on my achievements and give myself credit for my efforts.

39. I find strength in gratitude, even during difficult times.

40. I appreciate the moments of stillness that bring clarity.

41. I embrace the lessons learned from my past.

42. I am grateful for the opportunities to create meaningful memories.

43. I celebrate my uniqueness and all that I bring to the world.

44. I honor the connections I have built along my journey.

45. I practice introspection to enhance my gratitude.

46. I am thankful for the wisdom gained through life's experiences.

47. I recognize how far I have come and celebrate that progress.

48. I express gratitude for the love and joy in my life.

49. I appreciate the lessons that come from challenges.

50. I cultivate a habit of reflecting on my daily blessings.

51. I am grateful for the opportunities that lie ahead.

52. I take time to acknowledge my feelings and express gratitude.

53. I celebrate my effort and perseverance in reaching my goals.

54. I am thankful for the moments that bring me joy and happiness.

55. I recognize the beauty in each stage of my journey.

56. I express gratitude to myself for my hard work and dedication.

57. I find inspiration in the challenges I have overcome.

58. I appreciate the growth that comes from stepping outside my comfort zone.

59. I reflect on my day with gratitude and appreciation.

60. I am thankful for the ability to manifest my dreams.

61. I celebrate the people who have supported me along my journey.

62. I practice gratitude to enhance my overall well-being.

63. I cherish the experiences that have shaped my life and perspective.

64. I express appreciation for the lessons learned from failure.

65. I am thankful for the beauty and wonder of life.

66. I embrace every moment, knowing they contribute to my growth.

67. I recognize the power of gratitude to shift my mindset.

68. I am grateful for my ability to make positive choices.

69. I celebrate my creativity and the joy it brings me.

70. I appreciate the challenges that have taught me resilience.

71. I express gratitude for the strength I find within myself.

72. I take time to reflect on my journey and acknowledge my progress.

73. I am thankful for the peace that comes with gratitude.

74. I embrace the lessons of my past as gifts for my future.

75. I recognize the abundance present in my life.

76. I practice gratitude to cultivate joy and fulfillment.

77. I am thankful for the ability to create positive change in my life.

78. I am grateful for the moments that challenge me to grow.

79. I celebrate the achievements that I have worked hard for.

80. I take intentional time to reflect on my daily blessings.

81. I appreciate each step of my journey, knowing it shapes who I am.

82. I acknowledge the love and support I receive from those around me.

83. I find joy in the process, not just the outcome.

84. I express gratitude for my ability to create my own happiness.

85. I honor my progress and take pride in my accomplishments.

86. I am thankful for the lessons my experiences have imparted.

87. I practice gratitude to attract more positive experiences into my life.

88. I celebrate the small victories that contribute to my larger goals.

89. I embrace my journey with an open heart and a grateful spirit.

90. I appreciate the beauty in the everyday moments of life.

91. I reflect on my achievements with pride and appreciation.

92. I am grateful for the insights gained through self-reflection.

93. I acknowledge my strengths and the growth I have achieved.

94. I take a moment each day to express gratitude for my life.

95. I celebrate the people who inspire and motivate me.

96. I am thankful for new opportunities to grow and evolve.

97. I cherish the memories created with loved ones and friends.

98. I find gratitude even in the face of adversity.

99. I embrace the power of reflection to enhance my self-awareness.

100. I am grateful for the journey of becoming the

best version of myself.

# 11

## Enhancing Emotional Well-Being.

Affirmations that promote emotional intelligence, consciousness, and self-compassion, helping you navigate your feelings and cultivate a balanced emotional state.

# Chapter 11

## Enhancing Emotional Well-Being.

Affirmations that promote emotional intelligence, consciousness, and self-compassion, helping you navigate your feelings and cultivate a balanced emotional state.

In the complex rhythm of life, our emotional well-being serves as the foundation for our happiness, resilience, and personal fulfillment. Emotions are intricately woven into our experiences, influencing how we think, act, and relate to others. Acknowledging and nurturing our emotional health is essential for fostering a balanced mindset and fostering a fulfilled life.

In this chapter, you will discover a collection of affirmations designed to enhance your emotional well-being. These positive statements are meant to promote emotional intelligence, consciousness, and self-compassion, providing you with the tools to navigate your feelings with grace and understanding. By integrating these affirmations into your daily routine, you create a practice that encourages you to embrace your emotions rather than shy away from them.

Each affirmation serves as a gentle reminder that it is okay to feel and that every emotion, whether joyful or challenging, plays a significant role in our personal growth. By honoring your feelings and allowing yourself the space to process them, you cultivate a deeper awareness of your emotional landscape. This self-awareness is the catalyst for change, empowering you to respond mindfully to situations rather than react impulsively.

Practicing self-compassion is a key component of emotional well-being. It allows you to treat yourself with kindness and understanding, especially during difficult times. As you offer yourself grace in moments of struggle, you build resilience and foster a nurturing relationship with your inner self. This chapter encourages you to celebrate not only your successes but also your vulnerabilities, recognizing that both are integral to your journey.

As you engage with these affirmations, take the time to reflect on your emotional experiences and how they shape your perspective. Allow these positive statements to inspire and uplift you, transforming your relationship with your emotions. Let's embark on this journey of enhancing emotional well-being together, cultivating a mindset of love, compassion, and strength in the face of life's challenges!

1. I honor my emotions and allow myself to feel

without judgment.

2. I am in tune with my feelings and embrace them as part of me.

3. I practice focus, staying present in each moment.

4. I treat myself with kindness and compassion, especially during difficult times.

5. I acknowledge my struggles and give myself permission to heal.

6. I cultivate a deep sense of inner peace and calm.

7. I am resilient and capable of navigating my emotions.

8. I release negativity and embrace positive feelings.

9. I approach my emotions with curiosity and openness.

10. I express my feelings in healthy and constructive ways.

11. I am worthy of love and understanding, both from myself and others.

12. I celebrate the progress I make in managing my emotions.

13. I am learning to respond to my feelings with grace and patience.

14. I embrace vulnerability as a source of strength and connection.

15. I affirm my growth and emotional well-being every day.

16. I allow myself to rest and recharge when I need it.

17. I am grateful for the emotional insights I gain from my experiences.

18. I practice self-compassion and acknowledge my humanity.

19. I release the need to be perfect and accept myself as I am.

20. I find joy in the simple moments of life.

21. I create space for reflection and self-discovery.

22. My emotions do not define me; I am more than how I feel.

23. I seek support when I need it and embrace community.

24. I am deserving of happiness, love, and fulfillment.

25. I cultivate healthy coping mechanisms to manage my feelings.

26. I am proud of my ability to articulate my emotions.

27. I approach each day with an open heart and mind.

28. I find balance in my emotional responses.

29. I give myself permission to prioritize my mental well-being.

30. I embrace the journey of personal growth with self-compassion.

31. I nurture my emotional health with positivity and love.

32. I practice gratitude for the lessons my emotions teach me.

33. I am learning to be more self-aware in my emotional experiences.

34. I allow my feelings to guide me towards personal insight.

35. I choose to focus on what uplifts my spirit.

36. I am capable of turning negative emotions into learning opportunities.

37. I celebrate my emotional journey and the strength it brings.

38. I engage in activities that promote my emotional well-being.

39. I am worthy of investing time in my self-care.

40. I allow myself to express my emotions freely and authentically.

41. I embrace change as an essential part of my emotional growth.

42. I honor my boundaries and prioritize my emotional space.

43. I am committed to understanding my emotions and motivations.

44. I practice deep breathing to cultivate a sense of calm.

45. I choose to respond to challenges with a positive mindset.

46. I release guilt for prioritizing my emotional health.

47. I recognize the importance of self-reflection in fostering growth.

48. I am grateful for the supportive relationships in my life.

49. I find comfort in solitude and self-exploration.

50. I consciously choose love and compassion over fear and negativity.

51. I embrace my individuality while remaining connected to others.

52. I am open to learning from my emotions and experiences.

53. I allow myself to feel joy and express it fully.

54. I practice forgiveness towards myself and others.

55. I am committed to creating a harmonious inner dialogue.

56. I celebrate my unique emotional landscape and perspectives.

57. I cultivate patience as I navigate my feelings.

58. I am worthy of care and consideration from myself and others.

59. I approach my emotional health with curiosity and dedication.

60. I align my thoughts with love and understanding.

61. I seek joy in every experience, no matter how small.

62. I nurture my spirit with love and gratitude.

63. I let go of the past and embrace the present moment.

64. I plant seeds of positivity within my heart.

65. I am compassionate toward myself, especially during difficult emotions.

66. I am capable of creating peaceful moments in my life.

67. I engage in mindful practices that enhance my emotional well-being.

68. I acknowledge and honor my emotional needs.

69. I find strength in sharing my feelings with trusted individuals.

70. I am deserving of emotional healing and growth.

71. I cultivate a routine that supports my mental wellness.

72. I am in control of my emotional responses.

73. I take pride in my ability to understand my feelings.

74. I fill my mind with thoughts of love, peace, and positivity.

75. I am committed to connecting with my emotions each day.

76. I approach my feelings with gentleness and understanding.

77. I prioritize self-care and make time for activities that nourish my spirit.

78. I am resilient, strong, and capable of navigating life's challenges.

79. I choose to focus on the positive aspects of my life.

80. I embrace self-compassion, treating myself with the kindness I offer others.

81. I allow my emotions to flow freely without judgment.

82. I am grateful for the lessons that emotions can teach me.

83. I trust in my ability to adapt and grow through my experiences.

84. I surround myself with positive energy that uplifts my spirit.

85. I am worthy of a peaceful and happy life.

86. I take time to pause, breathe, and reconnect with my feelings.

87. I nurture my emotional health with practices that bring me joy.

88. I embrace any changes that support my emotional growth.

89. I celebrate my emotional journey and the growth it brings.

90. I am open to seeking guidance when I feel overwhelmed.

91. I practice awareness to cultivate greater self-awareness.

92. I am worthy of living a fulfilling, emotionally balanced life.

93. I forgive myself for past mistakes, allowing room for growth.

94. I share my thoughts and feelings with honesty and openness.

95. I prioritize my mental health as an important part of my well-being.

96. I am capable of overcoming emotional challenges with grace.

97. I cherish my relationships and nurture them with love.

98. I acknowledge my feelings as valid and important.

99. I carry gratitude in my heart, which enriches my life.

100. I take pride in my ability to express emotions authentically.

# 12

## Unlocking Your Innter Potential.

Positive affirmations aimet at recognizing and embracing your unique strengths and talents, empowering you to puruse your passions and dreams with confidence.

# Chapter 12

## Unlocking Your Inner Potential.

Positive affirmations aimed at recognizing and embracing your unique strengths and talents, empowering you to pursue you passions and dreams with confidence.

Each of us holds a unique set of strengths and talents that, when nurtured and embraced, have the power to transform our lives. Unlocking your inner potential is an empowering journey of self-discovery, where you learn to recognize and fully express your individuality. This chapter is dedicated to helping you tap into that potential, reminding you that you are worthy of pursuing your passions and dreams with confidence.

In a world that often encourages conformity, it can be easy to lose sight of what makes you special. This section highlights the importance of embracing your unique qualities and recognizing that they are your greatest assets. By repeating the affirmations within this chapter, you cultivate a mindset that honors your individuality and inspires you to believe in your capabilities.

These affirmations serve as guiding lights, encouraging you to confront self-doubt and fear while igniting the courage to take bold steps toward your aspirations. Each statement reinforces the understanding that challenges are not barriers but rather opportunities for growth and self-improvement. As you learn to view obstacles through this lens, you will discover that you possess the resilience needed to navigate life's complexities and pursue your true calling.

Furthermore, unlocking your inner potential is about more than just achieving personal success; it involves fostering a positive impact on the lives of others. By embracing your strengths and pursuing your passions wholeheartedly, you not only empower yourself but also inspire those around you to do the same.

As you engage with the affirmations in this chapter, take the time to reflect on your journey and the unique gifts you possess. Let these affirmations resonate within you, encouraging you to explore new paths, take risks, and celebrate every step of the way. Together, let's embark on this empowering journey of unlocking your inner potential, allowing your true self to shine and thrive!

1. I am worthy of pursuing my passions and dreams.

2. I embrace my unique strengths and talents with

pride.

3. I trust in my ability to achieve great things.

4. I am capable of transforming my dreams into

reality.

5. I unlock my potential by believing in myself.

6. I am open to discovering new talents within me.

7. I celebrate my individuality as my greatest asset.

8. I have the power to create the life I desire.

9. I trust myself to take bold steps toward my goals.

10. I am courageous and face challenges with confidence.

11. I nurture my creativity and let it flourish.

12. I am constantly growing and evolving into my best self.

13. I acknowledge my accomplishments and take pride in my journey.

14. I attract opportunities that align with my passions.

15. I am in tune with my intuition and guided by it.

16. I have the ability to overcome any obstacle I encounter.

17. I believe in my capacity for greatness.

18. I release self-doubt and embrace self-confidence.

19. I create a positive mindset that propels me forward.

20. I am worthy of success in all areas of my life.

21. I take inspired action to pursue my dreams.

22. I trust that my unique contributions are valuable.

23. I am resilient and bounce back stronger from setbacks.

24. I am surrounded by love and support as I pursue my goals.

25. I embrace challenges as opportunities for growth and learning.

26. I have the courage to step outside my comfort zone.

27. I acknowledge my strengths and use them to my advantage.

28. I find joy in pursuing my passions every day.

29. I am open to feedback and use it to improve myself.

30. I visualize my success and take steps toward it confidently.

31. I am capable of achieving anything I set my mind to.

32. I celebrate my individuality and the gifts I bring to the world.

33. I am passionate about my goals and pursue them wholeheartedly.

34. I trust the journey and remain patient with my progress.

35. I gather inspiration from my experiences and surroundings.

36. I am capable of creating positive change in my life.

37. I choose to believe in my abilities and potential.

38. I embrace my uniqueness and make it my strength.

39. I am committed to my personal growth and self-improvement.

40. I release limiting beliefs that hold me back from success.

41. I am deserving of all the good that life has to offer.

42. I tap into my creativity to solve problems and explore new ideas.

43. I invest time in nurturing my talents and passions.

44. I am grateful for the unique qualities that make me who I am.

45. I trust that I am on the right path to achieving my dreams.

46. I am open to learning from my experiences and mistakes.

47. I embrace the unknown as an opportunity for discovery.

48. I take pride in my accomplishments and the journey I have taken.

49. I affirm my abilities and pursue my dreams with confidence.

50. I am determined to turn my dreams into actionable goals.

51. I recognize the potential for greatness within me.

52. I cultivate a mindset of abundance and positivity.

53. I embrace the challenges that come with pursuing my passions.

54. I find strength in my ability to manifest my desires.

55. I trust that the universe supports me in my journey.

56. I release the fear of failure and embrace a growth mindset.

57. I celebrate each step I take toward my aspirations.

58. I am constantly learning and growing as an individual.

59. I trust my instincts and intuition in making decisions.

60. I am capable of inspiring others through my actions and words.

61. I nurture my dreams and work towards them every day.

62. I take responsibility for my happiness and success.

63. I find fulfillment in imperfect progress toward my goals.

64. I choose to surround myself with positivity and encouragement.

65. I recognize and embrace my worth in every situation.

66. I am open to new experiences that expand my horizons.

67. I celebrate the uniqueness of my journey and its lessons.

68. I have the strength to pursue my ambitions with commitment.

69. I trust myself to take the necessary risks for growth.

70. I acknowledge the power of my thoughts and actions.

71. I am capable of making a difference in the world.

72. I honor my values and align my actions with them.

73. I embrace the evolution of my passions as I grow.

74. I celebrate my creativity as a key part of my potential.

75. I am fearless in the pursuit of my dreams.

76. I recognize that setbacks are part of my growth journey.

77. I allow myself to feel empowered in every situation.

78. I attract positive energy that fuels my aspirations.

79. I allow myself to dream big and pursue those dreams boldly.

80. I am worthy of pursuing my dreams and ambitions.

81. I approach each day with renewed determination to succeed.

82. I celebrate my creativity and let it guide my journey.

83. I am open to discovering new paths and opportunities.

84. I have the strength to rise above challenges and thrive.

85. I trust that my unique voice adds value to the world.

86. I nurture my passions with dedication and focus.

87. I am committed to finding joy in my pursuits.

88. I choose to believe in my potential every day.

89. I embrace my individuality and let it inspire my actions.

90. I am constantly evolving and expanding my horizons.

91.   I trust that every step is leading me closer to my goals.

92.   I embody confidence and self-assurance in all I do.

93.   I find empowerment in pursuing my true calling.

94.   I recognize that my journey is uniquely mine and that's okay.

95.   I learn from others while embracing my unique path.

96.   I possess the determination to turn my dreams into reality.

97.   I allow my passions to guide my decisions and actions.

98.    I am grateful for the talents that make me who I am.

99.    I take meaningful action towards my aspirations daily.

100.    I embrace new challenges as opportunities to grow.

# 13

## Creating Harmonious Environments.

Affirmations designed to foster peace and harmony in your surroundings, encouraging you to cultivate a nurturing atmosphere that supports your well-being and creativity.

# Chapter 13

# Creating Harmonious Environments.

Affirmations designed to foster peace and harmony in your surroundings, encouraging you to cultivate a nurturing atmosphere that supports your well-being and creativity.

Our surroundings play a vital role in shaping our emotional state and overall well-being. The environment we create for ourselves and others significantly impacts our ability to thrive, grow, and express our creativity. When we cultivate a harmonious atmosphere, we foster peace, inspiration, and a sense of belonging that enriches our lives and the lives of those we interact with.

In this chapter, you will discover affirmations designed to help you create an environment that promotes tranquility and positivity. These affirmations serve as powerful tools to inspire you to nurture your surroundings with love and intention. By integrating these thoughts into your daily routine, you actively participate in shaping an environment that supports your well-being and personal growth.

Creating a harmonious environment goes beyond physical space—it's about cultivating an emotional landscape that fosters connections, creativity, and joy. The affirmations in this chapter encourage you to recognize the beauty in simplicity, embrace the power of observation, and actively seek to surround yourself with uplifting energy. By taking these steps, you create a nurturing atmosphere that allows your unique gifts to shine and your spirit to flourish.

As you engage with these affirmations, take a moment to reflect on the spaces you inhabit and the energy they bring to your life. Allow these positive statements to encourage you to express gratitude for the beauty within your surroundings and the potential they hold for inspired living. Let's embark on this journey together, creating harmonious environments that elevate our emotional well-being and inspire us to thrive!

1. I create a peaceful and nurturing environment around me.

2. My space reflects my intentions for calm and creativity.

3. I attract positive energy and serenity into my life.

4. I am surrounded by beauty and inspiration in my environment.

5. I choose to let go of clutter and create space for harmony.

6. I nourish my surroundings with love and care.

7. I am committed to maintaining a peaceful atmosphere.

8. I invite tranquility into my home and workspace.

9. I appreciate the beauty in simple and harmonious moments.

10. I cultivate an environment that supports my well-being.

11. I surround myself with uplifting and positive influences.

12. I create a sanctuary that promotes relaxation and creativity.

13. I welcome balance and harmony into every aspect of my life.

14. I am grateful for the peace that my environment brings me.

15. I choose to fill my space with things that inspire joy and calm.

16. I engage in practices that foster a peaceful mindset.

17. I nurture my space with positive thoughts and intentions.

18. I express gratitude for the beauty of my surroundings.

19. I invite nature into my life, enhancing my sense of peace.

20. I am open to creating harmonious relationships in my environment.

21. I prioritize harmony and respect in my interactions with others.

22. I take moments to breathe deeply and appreciate my surroundings.

23. I create mindful routines that foster inner peace.

24. I surround myself with colors and elements that bring me joy.

25. I celebrate the serenity that comes from a clean and organized space.

26. I let go of negativity and embrace positivity in my environment.

27. I maintain a balanced lifestyle that promotes well-being.

28. I create supportive spaces for creativity and inspiration to flourish.

29. I am intentional about the energy I bring into my surroundings.

30. I acknowledge and celebrate the harmony in my relationships.

31. I am deserving of a peaceful and harmonious environment.

32. I practice attention to enhance my connection with my space.

33. I cultivate connections with nature that enrich my well-being.

34. I share love and kindness with those I share my space with.

35. I embrace silence and stillness as sources of peace.

36. I find solace in nature, allowing it to restore my spirit.

37. I choose to create an environment that reflects my values and beliefs.

38. I express gratitude for the relationships that contribute to my happiness.

39. I open my heart to receiving and giving love in my surroundings.

40. I am capable of transforming challenges into opportunities for harmony.

41. I find joy in the little things within my environment.

42. I nourish my spirit by surrounding myself with positive energy.

43. I embrace change as a tool for creating a harmonious space.

44. I actively seek out opportunities to cultivate peace.

45. I am aware of the impact my environment has on my emotional state.

46. I am grateful for the comfort my home provides.

47. I create spaces that allow me to be my authentic self.

48. I celebrate the beauty of connection to others in my environment.

49. I intentionally foster harmony in my thoughts and words.

50. I let go of what no longer serves my peace and well-being.

51. I create joyful experiences that resonate within my environment.

52. I am aligned with the energy of love and harmony.

53. I trust that my surroundings can uplift and inspire me.

54. I embrace healthy boundaries that promote peace in my relationships.

55. I reaffirm my commitment to a nurturing and harmonious space.

56. I enjoy the process of creating an environment that reflects my essence.

57. I take time to recharge in my peaceful surroundings.

58. I fill my space with elements that bring me comfort and joy.

59. I choose to communicate with kindness and understanding.

60. I foster an atmosphere of encouragement and support.

61. I believe in the power of harmony to enrich my life.

62. I am mindful of the energy I contribute to my environment.

63. I celebrate the positive changes I create in my space.

64. I cultivate a sense of belonging in my environment.

65. I embrace the beauty of collaboration and teamwork.

66. I heighten my awareness of the peace around me.

67. I create a harmonious balance between work and rest.

68. I maintain a healthy lifestyle that supports my emotional well-being.

69. I lovingly arrange my surroundings to reflect calm and creativity.

70. I express my feelings honestly, helping to create harmony.

71. I celebrate the connections I have with like-minded individuals.

72. I release stress and tension, creating space for peace.

73. I appreciate the harmonious moments shared with loved ones.

74. I find strength in the community I create around me.

75. I invite love and harmony into every new endeavor.

76. I immerse myself in the beauty of each season, reflecting on nature's rhythms.

77. I am committed to creating safe spaces for myself and others.

78. I attract positive relationships that contribute to my well-being.

79. I nurture gratitude within my environment, creating joy everywhere I go.

80. I take time to appreciate the peaceful moments in my day.

81. I approach each space I inhabit with love and intention.

82. I allow my environment to inspire and uplift my spirit.

83. I express my creativity in my surroundings, making them uniquely mine.

84. I am committed to fostering a culture of respect and kindness.

85. I create harmonious spaces that reflect my dreams and aspirations.

86. I invite laughter and joy into my relationships and environment.

87. I honor my needs and create spaces that promote relaxation and comfort.

88. I generate an atmosphere of positivity that encourages growth.

89. I find clarity and focus in my harmonious surroundings.

90. I engage in practices that promote inner peace and tranquility.

91. I am grateful for the vibrant energy that fills my space.

92. I nurture my emotional well-being through harmonious interactions.

93. I am inspired to cultivate beauty in both my surroundings and my life.

94. I express love and appreciation for the people and spaces that surround me.

95. I create an environment that encourages open communication and understanding.

96. I surround myself with elements that promote serenity and joy.

97. I am capable of transforming negative energy into positive vibes.

98. I recognize the importance of creating a harmonious balance in my life.

99. I celebrate the diversity of my relationships and the love they bring.

100. I stay grounded and present, appreciating the harmony around me.

# 14

## Cultivating a Growth Mindset.

Positive affirmations focused on developing a mindset that embraces learning, adaptability, and curiosity, encouraging you to view challenges as opportunities for personal and professional development.

# Chapter 14

## Cultivating a Growth Mindset.

Positive affirmations focused on developing a mindset that embraces learning, adaptability, and curiosity, encouraging you to view challenges as opportunities for personal and professional development.

The journey toward personal and professional fulfillment is paved with challenges, opportunities, and growth. Adopting a growth mindset is essential for navigating this journey, as it empowers us to view obstacles as valuable lessons rather than insurmountable barriers. A growth mindset fosters resilience, curiosity, and adaptability, allowing us to embrace change and pursue our passions with confidence.

In this chapter, you will find powerful affirmations designed to help you cultivate a growth mindset. These positive statements serve as reminders that our abilities and intelligence can be developed through dedication, effort, and perseverance. By integrating these affirmations into your daily life, you will reinforce the belief that you have the potential to learn, grow, and achieve your goals.

Cultivating a growth mindset means embracing challenges, celebrating progress, and recognizing that every experience contributes to our personal development. Each affirmation encourages you to approach setbacks with resilience and to remain open to the lessons and insights that accompany them. When you adopt this mindset, you empower yourself to take bold steps toward your aspirations, transforming fear and self-doubt into motivation and clarity.

Additionally, a growth mindset enhances your emotional well-being, allowing you to develop emotional intelligence and a greater understanding of your feelings. By acknowledging your strengths and weaknesses, you can make informed choices that align with your personal values and goals.

As you engage with the affirmations in this chapter, take the time to reflect on your journey and envision the possibilities that lie ahead. Allow these affirmations to inspire you to embrace learning, foster curiosity, and pursue your dreams with unwavering confidence. Together, let's embark on this transformative journey of cultivating a growth mindset, unlocking your inner potential, and celebrating the incredible progress that comes with it!

1. I embrace challenges as opportunities for growth

and learning.

2. I am open to new ideas and perspectives that

expand my understanding.

3. I view failures as valuable lessons that contribute to my development.

4. I am committed to lifelong learning and personal growth.

5. I celebrate my progress, knowing it is part of my journey.

6. I approach obstacles with curiosity and a willingness to learn.

7. I trust in my ability to adapt and thrive in any situation.

8. I seek feedback as a tool for improvement and growth.

9. I am resilient, bouncing back from setbacks with newfound strength.

10. I explore new possibilities, welcoming change in my life.

11. I recognize that my abilities can be developed through effort and practice.

12. I am excited about the process of learning and evolving.

13. I cultivate a mindset that embraces curiosity and exploration.

14. I am open to stepping outside my comfort zone for growth.

15. I believe in my potential to achieve greatness through learning.

16. I acknowledge that growth takes time, and I am patient with myself.

17. I am inspired by the growth of others and learn from their journeys.

18. I embrace feedback and use it to enhance my skills and abilities.

19. I am dedicated to setting and achieving personal and professional goals.

20. I trust that each experience, good or bad, contributes to my growth.

21. I approach new challenges with enthusiasm and courage.

22. I take pride in my ability to learn from mistakes and adapt accordingly.

23. I nurture a positive attitude that fosters growth and resilience.

24. I allow myself to be a beginner, knowing that growth takes practice.

25. I find joy in the journey of self-improvement and exploration.

26. I celebrate my unique path and the lessons it brings.

27. I am open to change, knowing it can lead to exciting new opportunities.

28. I trust in my capacity to navigate challenges with grace.

29. I cultivate a mindset that encourages creativity and innovation.

30. I recognize that learning and growth are lifelong endeavors.

31. I empower myself to take risks that lead to personal development.

32. I am capable of turning challenges into stepping stones for success.

33. I embrace the discomfort that comes with growth as a sign of progress.

34. I am constantly evolving and adapting to new circumstances.

35. I view criticism as constructive feedback that helps me improve.

36. I believe that every challenge I face is a chance to expand my skills.

37. I am committed to my personal development journey and take intentional steps forward.

38. I surround myself with people who encourage and inspire growth.

39. I let go of limiting beliefs and embrace a mindset of possibility.

40. I am capable of reinventing myself and my goals at any time.

41. I approach life with wonder and a desire to learn from every experience.

42. I appreciate the value of persistence and hard work in achieving growth.

43. I trust that my potential is limitless and always expanding.

44. I recognize and embrace my strengths, using them to overcome challenges.

45. I approach learning with an open heart and a willing spirit.

46. I am inspired by my journey and the progress I continue to make.

47. I understand that growth often requires stepping into the unknown.

48. I honor my successes and learn from my failures with grace.

49. I practice self-compassion as I navigate the ups and downs of growth.

50. I make time for self-reflection and personal growth each day.

51. I celebrate the journey, knowing that each step is important.

52. I am eager to embrace new challenges with confidence.

53. I trust the process of growth and remain open to the lessons it brings.

54. I believe that my hard work and dedication will yield positive results.

55. I actively seek opportunities for learning in every situation.

56. I have the resilience to face any challenge that comes my way.

57. I choose to cultivate a mindset filled with positivity and hope.

58. I acknowledge my progress and share my journey with pride.

59. I am patient with myself and trust that growth takes time.

60. I embrace uncertainty as a catalyst for transformation and growth.

61. I am dedicated to nourishing my mind and expanding my skills.

62. I find inspiration in the stories of others who have grown through adversity.

63. I am open to new challenges, ready to embrace learning opportunities.

64. I view obstacles as opportunities to become stronger and wiser.

65. I value my unique perspective and trust in my creative insights.

66. I am committed to nurturing a mindset of exploration and curiosity.

67. I am always striving to become the best version of myself.

68. I take deliberate steps toward my goals, no matter how small.

69. I embrace challenges as valuable pathways to growth.

70. I am open to constructive criticism as a means of improvement.

71. I believe that effort and perseverance lead to success.

72. I cultivate curiosity about the world around me.

73. I am willing to leave my comfort zone to pursue my dreams.

74. I am grateful for the opportunities that help me learn and grow.

75. I acknowledge the progress I've made and look forward to what's next.

76. I surround myself with positive influences that encourage my growth.

77. I embrace setbacks as chances to learn and adapt.

78. I am patient with my progress and trust my journey.

79. I recognize that every experience contributes to my development.

80. I am capable of making positive changes in my life.

81. I actively seek out learning opportunities in my daily life.

82. I am excited to discover new aspects of myself along the way.

83. I celebrate the efforts I make toward my personal reflection.

84. I am aligned with my purpose, guiding me on my growth journey.

85. I recognize the importance of self-discipline in achieving my goals.

86. I approach new challenges with confidence and enthusiasm.

87. I am open to the lessons that failure can teach me.

88. I invest time in my personal and professional development.

89. I embrace collaboration and learn from others' perspectives.

90. I trust that I am capable of adapting to any situation.

91. I actively seek feedback to enhance my growth experience.

92. I celebrate my curiosity and desire to learn every day.

93. I am fearless in exploring the possibilities that lie ahead.

94. I am willing to explore different approaches to reach my goals.

95. I stay focused on my growth journey, regardless of distractions.

96. I visualize my success and take actionable steps toward it.

97. I commit to learning from my experiences, both positive and negative.

98. I have the power within me to create the change I desire.

99. I approach my dreams with a sense of adventure and wonder.

100. I am grateful for my ability to adapt and grow through life's experiences.

# 15

## Celebrating Love and Life.

Affirmations of appreciation and thankfulness.

# Chapter 15

# Celebrating Love and Life.

## Affirmations of Appreciation and Thankfulness.

Love is a powerful force that enriches our lives, connects us to others, and provides us with a profound sense of purpose and belonging. It is often said that love is the greatest gift we can give and receive, and when we cultivate an appreciation for love and the joys of life, we unlock a deeper understanding of ourselves and the world around us. This chapter is dedicated to embracing that love and joy through the practice of gratitude and appreciation.

In "Celebrating Love and Life," you will encounter a collection of affirmations that encourage you to cultivate an attitude of thankfulness and recognition for the beauty that surrounds you. Each affirmation serves as a reminder to pause, reflect, and appreciate the love that graces your life, whether it comes from family, friends, or the simple joys of everyday existence. By consciously acknowledging the positive aspects of your life, you invite more abundance and fulfillment into your experience.

The act of celebrating life and love fosters emotional well-being and resilience. When we focus on gratitude, we shift our perspective from what we lack to what we have, creating a mindset that is open to joy and positivity. This chapter encourages you to express love not only to others but also to yourself—recognizing that self-love is the foundation upon which healthy relationships are built.

As you engage with the affirmations in this chapter, allow yourself to fully embrace the richness of your experiences and the connections that make life meaningful. Celebrate both the grand moments and the everyday acts of kindness that fill your heart with warmth. Let these positive words inspire you to express appreciation, cultivate joy, and celebrate the extraordinary beauty of love and life every day.

Together, let's embark on this journey of celebration, recognizing that each moment holds the potential for gratitude and joy, reminding us of the incredible tapestry of love that weaves through our lives!

1. I am grateful for the love that surrounds me every

day.

2. I cherish the beauty of life and all its experiences.

3. I celebrate the relationships that bring joy to my

life.

4. I appreciate the little things that make each day special.

5. I am thankful for the support and kindness of my loved ones.

6. I find joy in both the highs and lows of my journey.

7. I embrace love in all its forms and expressions.

8. I am grateful for the lessons life has taught me.

9. I radiate love and positivity to those around me.

10. I celebrate my unique journey and the experiences that shape me.

11. I appreciate the present moment and all it has to offer.

12. I express gratitude for my health and well-being.

13. I honor the people in my life who inspire me.

14. I find beauty in everyday moments of love and connection.

15. I embrace joy and happiness as integral parts of my life.

16. I am thankful for the opportunities that allow me to grow.

17. I recognize and celebrate the love I have for myself.

18. I create space for gratitude and appreciation in my heart.

19. I cherish the memories made with friends and family.

20. I am grateful for the abundance present in my life.

21. I express love openly and honestly to those I care about.

22. I celebrate the milestones in my life, big and small.

23. I appreciate the moments of laughter and joy shared with others.

24. I take time to reflect on my journey and express gratitude.

25. I welcome new connections and experiences that enrich my life.

26. I am thankful for the comfort and security my relationships provide.

27. I celebrate the diverse expressions of love in the world.

28. I embrace every moment as a gift worth cherishing.

29. I cultivate an attitude of gratitude in all areas of my life.

30. I celebrate my achievements and the journey that brings them to life.

31. I appreciate the beauty of nature and its ability to uplift my spirit.

32. I honor my emotions and express them with love.

33. I find inspiration in the love I see around me.

34. I am grateful for the ability to share my life with others.

35. I celebrate the growth that comes from overcoming challenges.

36. I acknowledge the abundance of love in my life.

37. I express my gratitude to the universe for the blessings I receive.

38. I cultivate loving thoughts towards myself and others.

39. I recognize the importance of kindness and compassion in my life.

40. I celebrate the connections that uplift and inspire me.

41. I appreciate the safety and comfort of my home and loved ones.

42. I embrace the journey of love as a continuous adventure.

43. I find peace in expressing my authentic self in my relationships.

44. I am thankful for every opportunity to connect with others.

45. I celebrate my individuality and the love I bring to the world.

46. I express gratitude for the lessons learned from every experience.

47. I let love guide my interactions and decisions each day.

48. I appreciate the simple joys of life that fill my heart with warmth.

49. I acknowledge the sacrifices made by others who love me.

50. I find strength in vulnerability and openness in relationships.

51. I elevate those around me through my words and actions.

52. I celebrate my emotional growth and the love I have cultivated within.

53. I appreciate moments of stillness that allow me to reflect.

54. I express love and appreciation freely to those I care about.

55. I nurture a spirit of gratitude that enhances my life experience.

56. I take time to celebrate my journey with joy and reflection.

57. I acknowledge the love I receive and give with an open heart.

58. I celebrate the kindness of others and reciprocate it generously.

59. I am thankful for the laughter and joy shared with friends and family.

60. I cherish the connection I have to my community and the world.

61. I am open to receiving love in all its forms.

62. I take joy in the relationships that inspire my personal growth.

63. I find beauty in the imperfections of life and love.

64. I appreciate the moments of love that touch my heart deeply.

65. I express gratitude for the experiences that shape my perspective.

66. I celebrate the diversity of love and the joy it brings.

67. I am thankful for the ability to bring happiness to others.

68. I honor the lessons learned from love's challenges.

69. I am thankful for each day, and I embrace the love and joy it brings into my life.

70. I embrace each day as a new opportunity to share love and gratitude.

71. I express appreciation for the kindness I receive from others.

72. I am grateful for the unique relationships that enrich my life.

73. I find joy in the connections I make with others around me.

74. I acknowledge the power of love to heal and transform.

75. I celebrate the moments of stillness that allow for reflection.

76. I am thankful for the spontaneity that brings joy to my life.

77. I nurture my heart by surrounding myself with positive, loving people.

78. I make time for love in both my personal and professional life.

79. I appreciate the laughter that fills my life with joy.

80. I open my heart to the beauty of friendship and camaraderie.

81. I cherish the lessons that love teaches me each day.

82. I embrace every opportunity to express my love and appreciation.

83. I am grateful for my ability to give love freely and openly.

84. I celebrate the little acts of kindness that create lasting memories.

85. I acknowledge the love I have for myself as a foundation for healthy relationships.

86. I find magic in the everyday moments shared with loved ones.

87. I appreciate the safety and comfort that comes from loving relationships.

88. I honor and value the time spent with those I care for.

89. I am grateful for the unconditional love that surrounds me.

90. I open my heart to forgiveness, releasing negativity and hurt.

91. I celebrate the bonds I share with my family and friends.

92. I am thankful for the love that supports my growth and healing.

93. I take a moment each day to reflect on my blessings and express gratitude.

94. I find joy in simple pleasures and everyday moments of love.

95. I cherish the meaningful conversations that deepen my connections.

96. I express love through my words, actions, and intentions.

97. I am grateful for the lessons learned through love and relationships.

98. I embrace the journey of love with an open heart and mind.

99. I honor the impact that love has on my life and choices.

100. I celebrate the gift of life and the relationships

that make it meaningful.

# EPILOGUE

**The Journey Continues.**

# EPILOGUE

## The Journey Continues.

As we reach the end of this exploration into the power of positive affirmations, it's essential to remember that the journey of self-discovery, growth, and positivity is ongoing. The affirmations presented throughout this book are not mere words; they are powerful tools that can transform your mindset and enhance your life. Each affirmation you have engaged with has the potential to ignite change, inspire confidence, and foster resilience.

The practice of affirmations invites you to cultivate a deeper connection with yourself and your aspirations. It encourages you to embrace your individuality, cherish your journey, and recognize the abundance that exists within and around you. While this book serves as a guide, the real magic happens when you take these affirmations into your daily life, making them a part of your routine and allowing them to shape your thoughts, beliefs, and actions.

You may encounter moments of doubt or setbacks along the way, but know that these experiences are a natural part of your journey. The resilience you have cultivated through these affirmations will empower you to rise above challenges and continue moving forward. Each day presents a new opportunity to reaffirm your commitment to self-love, gratitude, creativity, and connection.

As you move beyond the pages of this book, I encourage you to remain open to the infinite possibilities life has to offer. Embrace change, seek out new beginnings, and foster meaningful relationships with others. Continue to use affirmations as a source of inspiration and motivation, allowing them to guide you toward a life filled with purpose, joy, and fulfillment.

Thank you for engaging in this journey of self-discovery and empowerment. Remember, you have the power within you to create the life you desire—one that is abundant with love, success, and personal growth. Keep nurturing your mind with positivity and embrace every step of your path ahead. Your journey is just beginning, and the best is yet to come!

# 1500 POSITIVE AFFIRMATIONS FOR WOMEN AND MEN:

## Take advantage of the power of positive thinking, attract money, happiness, love and success.

This book would not have come to life without the invaluable support and inspiration of many remarkable individuals. I am profoundly grateful to my family and friends for their unwavering encouragement and belief in my vision. A special thanks goes to my mentors and fellow creators who have shared their insights and experiences, shaping my understanding of personal growth and the power of positive affirmations. I am also indebted to the countless readers who have shared their stories of resilience and transformation, reminding me of the profound impact that cultivating a positive mindset can have on our lives.

I wrote this book with a singular vision: to empower individuals on their journey towards self-acceptance, fulfillment, and growth. In a world that often challenges our self-worth and encourages negativity, I recognized the need for a resource that not only highlights the importance of self-affirmations but also fosters a culture of gratitude and positivity. Our aim is to equip you with nurturing and uplifting affirmations that inspire personal expression, creativity, and emotional well-being.

By integrating these affirmations into daily life, we hope to foster a transformative mindset that allows everyone to embrace their uniqueness, overcome challenges, and pursue their passions with confidence. Together, let us create a life filled with joy, abundance, and purpose, and celebrate the beauty of our individual journeys!

*"I am a magnet for abundance, happiness, love, and success. Every day, I attract prosperous opportunities and positive energies into my life. I am worthy of all the good things I aspire to, and I thank God for the endless blessings flowing to me now. I am grateful for this moment of growth and transformation. Thank you, God, for opening my heart to limitless possibilities."*

www.ingramcontent.com/pod-product-compliance
Lightning Source LLC
Chambersburg PA
CBHW061818040426

42447CB00012B/2712

*9798899651335*